THE NEW COLLEGEVILLE BIBLE COMMENTARY

SIRACH

Jeremy Corley

SERIES EDITOR

Daniel Durken, O.S.B.

LITURGICAL PRESS

Collegeville, Minnesota

www.litpress.org

Nihil Obstat: Reverend Robert Harren, *Censor deputatus*.
Imprimatur: ✠ Most Reverend John F. Kinney, J.C.D., D.D., Bishop of St. Cloud,
      Minnesota, April 15, 2013.

Design by Ann Blattner.

Cover illustration: Detail of *Praise of Wisdom* by Suzanne Moore. © 2007 *The Saint John's Bible*, Saint John's Univerity, Collegeville, Minnesota. Used with permission. All rights reserved.

Photos: page 10, Wikimedia Commons; pages 52, 61, 70, and 122, Thinkstock Photos.

1	2	3	4	5	6	7	8	9

Library of Congress Cataloging-in-Publication Data

Corley, Jeremy.
      Sirach / Jeremy Corley.
            p.   cm. — (New Collegeville Bible commentary. Old Testament ; v.21)
      ISBN 978-0-8146-2855-3
      1. Bible. O.T. Apocrypha. Ecclesiasticus—Commentaries.   I. Title.

   BS1765.53.C67 2012
   229'.4077—dc23

                                                            2012035485

CONTENTS

Books of the Bible

Acts—Acts of the Apostles
Amos—Amos
Bar—Baruch
1 Chr—1 Chronicles
2 Chr—2 Chronicles
Col—Colossians
1 Cor—1 Corinthians
2 Cor—2 Corinthians
Dan—Daniel
Deut—Deuteronomy
Eccl (or Qoh)—Ecclesiastes
Eph—Ephesians
Esth—Esther
Exod—Exodus
Ezek—Ezekiel
Ezra—Ezra
Gal—Galatians
Gen—Genesis
Hab—Habakkuk
Hag—Haggai
Heb—Hebrews
Hos—Hosea
Isa—Isaiah
Jas—James
Jdt—Judith
Jer—Jeremiah
Job—Job
Joel—Joel
John—John
1 John—1 John
2 John—2 John
3 John—3 John
Jonah—Jonah
Josh—Joshua
Jude—Jude
Judg—Judges
1 Kgs—1 Kings

2 Kgs—2 Kings
Lam—Lamentations
Lev—Leviticus
Luke—Luke
1 Macc—1 Maccabees
2 Macc—2 Maccabees
Mal—Malachi
Mark—Mark
Matt—Matthew
Mic—Micah
Nah—Nahum
Neh—Nehemiah
Num—Numbers
Obad—Obadiah
1 Pet—1 Peter
2 Pet—2 Peter
Phil—Philippians
Phlm—Philemon
Prov—Proverbs
Ps(s)—Psalms
Rev—Revelation
Rom—Romans
Ruth—Ruth
1 Sam—1 Samuel
2 Sam—2 Samuel
Sir—Sirach
Song—Song of Songs
1 Thess—1 Thessalonians
2 Thess—2 Thessalonians
1 Tim—1 Timothy
2 Tim—2 Timothy
Titus—Titus
Tob—Tobit
Wis—Wisdom
Zech—Zechariah
Zeph—Zephaniah

The Book of Sirach

Title and author

The author's Hebrew name is Yeshua Ben (son of) Sira, which in the Greek translation became Jesus son of Sirach (50:27). Hence in Hebrew the book is known as the Wisdom of Ben Sira, and in Greek as Sirach. In Latin the work is called Liber Ecclesiasticus (the church book), because in the early Christian centuries it was widely used for instructing converts. This commentary employs the name Ben Sira for the author, and Sirach for the book.

Ben Sira composed his Hebrew work in Jerusalem, which plays a central role in his writing. He describes wisdom coming to dwell in Jerusalem (24:10-11) and pleads for divine mercy on the holy city (36:18-19). Furthermore, his depiction of the temple liturgy under the high priest Simeon II (50:5-21) appears to be the work of an eyewitness.

Ben Sira probably ran some kind of educational establishment in the city (51:23), though scholars dispute exactly when schools arose in ancient Israel. It is possible that Ben Sira was one of the "scribes of the temple" mentioned by Josephus (*Antiquities* 12.3.3 #142). The description of the scribe in 39:1-11 provides a kind of self-portrait of the author.

Date and place of composition

Scholars agree that Ben Sira's book dates from 195–175 B.C. Because the poem praising the high priest Simeon II speaks of him in the past tense (50:1-4), it must have been completed after his death around 196 B.C. Moreover, the Greek prologue speaks of the arrival of Ben Sira's grandson in Egypt in 132 B.C., which suggests that the author was active about half a century earlier. Additionally, there is no indication of the religious turmoil that followed the accession of the Seleucid king Antiochus IV Epiphanes, who reigned from 175 to 164 B.C. (1 Macc 1:10-64). Thus we may estimate Ben Sira to have been born soon after 250 B.C. and to have died around 175 B.C.

Throughout the sage's lifetime, the Holy Land was under the control of Greek-speaking rulers, first the Ptolemies of Egypt until the Battle of

Panium (200 B.C.), and then the Seleucids of Syria. For most of that time the people of Jerusalem were heavily taxed, though a decree of the Seleucid king Antiochus III (around 198 B.C.) reduced the city's tax burden for a while (Josephus, *Antiquities* 12.3.3-4 ##138-146). Since Greek language and culture were dominant in civic life, some Jews wishing for social advancement were tempted to abandon their ancestral faith and instead seek favor from the pagan authorities.

Canonical status

The grandson's Greek translation of the book was included in the Septuagint, which became the Bible of the early Greek-speaking church. From there it was translated into Latin. Its canonicity for Roman Catholics was defined at the Council of Trent (1546), whereas many Protestant reformers followed St. Jerome and the rabbinic tradition in rejecting it as uncanonical. The fact that the Greek version of the work became popular in the Christian Church may have contributed to its dropping out of usage in rabbinic Judaism. According to the Jerusalem Talmud (tractate *Sanhedrin* 28a), its use was excluded by Rabbi Akiba (d. ca. A.D. 132).

Because some rabbis spoke against the book, the Hebrew text almost vanished, except for a few proverbs quoted in rabbinic writings. Nevertheless, ancient Jewish respect for the book is evident from the Hebrew copies that have survived. The Dead Sea sites of Qumran and Masada have yielded some Hebrew fragments from before A.D. 70. Other Hebrew manuscripts from the tenth to the twelfth centuries A.D., copied by a group of non-rabbinic Jews called Karaites, were preserved in the storeroom (Genizah) of a Cairo synagogue. In all, the surviving Hebrew fragments cover two-thirds of the book.

Greek and Latin additions

Over time, scribes copying the Greek and Latin versions added supplementary lines, which often came to be added to the verse numbering. For example, some Greek manuscripts of the opening poem (1:1-10) include additions, which many modern translations place in footnotes or omit. The New American Bible has left out all these additions from the main text.

Because the Second Vatican Council urged Catholics to return to the original scriptural texts (*Dei Verbum* 22), the New American Bible has omitted material that seems like later Christian (or Jewish) scribal additions or changes, made to "improve" or "update" Ben Sira's teaching. One example concerns the afterlife. Like other Hebrew biblical authors before him (Isa 38:18; Pss 6:6; 115:17), Ben Sira had no clear expectation of the afterlife (10:11; 17:27-28). Thus, the Hebrew text of 7:17 says: "More and more, humble your pride; / what awaits mortals is worms." To bring in a reference here to punishment after death, the Greek translation reads: "The punishment of the impious is fire and worms."

Place in the wisdom tradition

The ancient Near East had a long tradition of scribal education, especially in Egypt. Wisdom literature is the term used to denote texts probing philosophical questions or offering advice on how to behave. Hebrew wisdom literature includes the behavioral admonitions of the book of Proverbs and the search into life's mysteries provided in the book of Job. Closer in time to Ben Sira, the skeptical author of Ecclesiastes sought a purpose in life, while after Ben Sira's time the writer of the book of Wisdom adapted traditional Israelite insights for a Greek-speaking audience. Like the book of Proverbs, Sirach consists entirely of poetry, except for the grandson's prologue.

Sources

Ben Sira's ideas and language suggest familiarity with earlier biblical writings. For instance, the Praise of the Ancestors (44:1–50:24) makes numerous allusions to the Hebrew Scriptures, while many of the ethical sayings develop thoughts found in the book of Proverbs. Because Ben Sira builds on the teaching of previous biblical authors, the commentary provides many cross-references to other scriptural texts. References not naming the book are to Sirach.

It is likely that Ben Sira also had some direct or indirect knowledge of some non-Jewish ancient writings. For instance, 38:24-34 adapts an ancient Egyptian wisdom theme, the *Satire of the Trades*, while other passages echo the thought of a sixth-century B.C. Greek poet named Theognis.

Structure

Whereas most of the book of Proverbs consists of diverse aphorisms, the outer sections (Prov 1:1–9:18 and 30:1–31:31) are comprised of longer poems. Ben Sira's book is generally made up of longer passages on a particular theme. Significant for the structure of his book are eight poems focusing on finding wisdom (1:1-10; 4:11-19; 6:18-37; 14:20–15:10; 24:1-33; 32:14–33:18; 38:24–39:11; 42:15–43:33). Many scholars regard these poems as introducing the eight major sections of 1:1–50:24.

Influence on the New Testament

Ben Sira had a widespread, though often indirect, influence on the New Testament. Thus, Matthew's sermon on the church calls for humility, offers advice on fraternal correction, and appeals for forgiveness (Matt 18:4, 15-17,

21-35), echoing three themes of Ben Sira (3:17-18; 19:13-17; 27:30–28:7). Luke's parables of the rich fool and the unjust judge (Luke 12:16-21; 18:1-8) develop ideas found in Ben Sira (11:18-19; 35:17-21). Finally, the letter of James treats topics like divine testing and control of the tongue (Jas 1:12-15; 3:1-12) that already occur in Ben Sira (2:1-6; 5:9-14).

Problems for modern readers

Over and above Christian reservations about Ben Sira's lack of belief in the afterlife, modern readers may well question some of the sage's attitudes, which were often based on social views from his time. Most regrettably, he exhibits prejudice against women (25:13-26). His misogyny builds on warnings in ancient wisdom literature addressed to young men about the allures of women (Prov 5:1-14; 7:6-27). His attitude may be explained (but not excused) by his professional setting in the shadow of the male-dominated Jerusalem temple, while an additional factor influencing him was the exclusion of women from many aspects of Greek civic life.

Sirach

Foreword

Inasmuch as many and great truths have been given to us through the Law, the prophets, and the authors who followed them, for which the instruction and wisdom of Israel merit praise, it is the duty of those who read the scriptures not only to become knowledgeable themselves but also to use their love of learning in speech and in writing to help others less familiar. So my grandfather Jesus, who had long devoted himself to the study of the law, the prophets, and the rest of the books of our ancestors, and had acquired great familiarity with them, was moved to write something himself regarding instruction and wisdom. He did this so that those who love learning might, by accepting what he had written, make even greater progress in living according to the Law.

GRANDSON'S PROLOGUE

Ben Sira's grandson supplied a prologue to his Greek translation of his grandfather's Hebrew work, just as Luke provided a prologue to the third gospel (Luke 1:1-4).

In the first paragraph, the grandson adopts a division of the Hebrew Bible into three parts, matching the subsequent rabbinic classification of law, prophets, and writings (compare Luke 24:44).

You are invited therefore to read it with good will and attention, with indulgence for any failure on our part, despite earnest efforts, in the interpretation of particular passages. For words spoken originally in Hebrew do not have the same effect when they are translated into another language. That is true not only of this book but of the Law itself, the prophecies, and the rest of the books, which differ no little when they are read in the original.

I arrived in Egypt in the thirty-eighth year of the reign of King Euergetes, and while there, I had access to no little learning. I therefore considered it my duty to devote some diligence and industry to the translation of this book. During this time I applied my skill for many sleepless hours to complete the book and publish it for those living abroad who wish to acquire learning and are disposed to live their lives according to the Law.

Because those who love learning have the duty to teach what they have learned (39:8), Yeshua Ben Sira (in Greek: Jesus son of Sirach) composed his book for the benefit of others (33:18). His purpose was that his audience would not feel pressured to seek wisdom in pagan Greek culture, but would remain steadfast in following the law of Moses (2:15-16; 42:1-2).

In the prologue's second paragraph, the grandson frankly admits the difficulty of translating from Hebrew to Greek, and there are many cases in Sirach where the Greek translation differs from the Hebrew (see notes on 4:10; 7:17; 48:11; 50:24). He is aware of the early Greek versions of several books of the Hebrew Bible. These translations, known as the Septuagint, were made in Alexandria in the third and second centuries B.C.

The prologue's third paragraph recounts the grandson's work of translation. The thirty-eighth year of the Egyptian king Ptolemy VII, known as Physcon Euergetes II, was 132 B.C. After his arrival in Egypt (presumably Alexandria) the translator found a copy of some valuable teaching, perhaps biblical books in Greek or other wisdom writings. Thereupon he felt obliged to translate his grandfather's work into Greek, not least because Alexandria had many thousands of Greek-speaking Jews.

The grandson's "many sleepless hours" may have covered more than fifteen years, since the Greek of the final paragraph suggests that King Euergetes (d. 117 B.C.) was already dead when the prologue was written. "Those living abroad" refers to the Jews dispersed outside Palestine, including those in Egypt.

11

Artistic depiction of Sirach by Engelhard Nunzer (Nuremberg, 1720).

The Wisdom of Ben Sira

God's Gift of Wisdom

1 ¹All wisdom is from the Lord
and remains with him forever.
²The sands of the sea, the drops of
rain,
the days of eternity—who can
count them?
³Heaven's height, earth's extent,
the abyss and wisdom—who can
explore them?
⁴Before all other things wisdom was
created;
and prudent understanding,
from eternity.

⁶The root of wisdom—to whom has
it been revealed?
Her subtleties—who knows
them?
⁸There is but one, wise and truly
awesome,
seated upon his throne—the
Lord.
⁹It is he who created her,
saw her and measured her,
Poured her forth upon all his works,
¹⁰upon every living thing according to his bounty,
lavished her upon those who
love him.

UNDERSTANDING WISDOM

Sirach 1:1—4:10

1:1-10 Where to find wisdom

Ben Sira begins his book with a clear assertion: wisdom is not primarily an achievement of human endeavor, but rather a gift from God (1 Kgs 3:9; Wis 9:1-4).

In Ben Sira's time, the cosmological questions of 1:2-3 were important, because of a double threat to Israel's traditional faith in the one Creator. The twin worldviews threatening traditional Judaism were the apocalyptic speculations of esoteric Jewish circles and the intellectual currents of Greek philosophy. In this context, Ben Sira's intention was that investigation of the world should be undertaken with a humble attitude toward God, based on an acceptance of divine revelation in the Torah (39:6-8).

Ben Sira views wisdom as preceding all creation (1:4), while other texts equate the divine wisdom with God's creative word (Ps 33:6; Prov 3:19). Having been formed by the Creator (Prov 8:22), wisdom is not a goddess or source of creation in place of the one God. The main text does not have 1:5 or 1:7, because these verses are later scribal additions, not found in the earliest manuscripts.

The question about where to locate wisdom (1:6) finds an answer in 1:8-10. Ben Sira directs his students' attention to the Lord, who is both wise and to be feared (Prov 1:7; 2:6). Since God measured out wisdom originally

Fear of the Lord Is Wisdom

¹¹The fear of the Lord is glory and
exultation,
gladness and a festive crown.
¹²The fear of the Lord rejoices the
heart,
giving gladness, joy, and long
life.
¹³Those who fear the Lord will be
happy at the end,
even on the day of death they
will be blessed.

¹⁴The beginning of wisdom is to
fear the Lord;
she is created with the faithful
in the womb.

¹⁵With the godly she was created
from of old,
and with their descendants she
will keep faith.

¹⁶The fullness of wisdom is to fear
the Lord;
she inebriates them with her
fruits.
¹⁷Their entire house she fills with
choice foods,
their granaries with her produce.

¹⁸The crown of wisdom is the fear
of the Lord,
flowering with peace and perfect
health.

---

in the Creation (Job 28:27), the best way to find wisdom is to be attentive to God the Creator.

Though wisdom is in principle accessible to all humanity, God gives it especially to "those who love him" (1:10). While this phrase could apply to anyone, it alludes especially to Moses' great commandment to Israel in the *Shema*: "You shall love the Lord, your God" (Deut 6:5). Here, therefore, it may refer particularly to Israel, which had been commanded to love God.

Besides intellectual knowledge, wisdom also involves the practical action of keeping the Torah (Deut 4:6). Thus, the poem that began with a universal scope (heaven, earth, the abyss) ends with a special focus on Israel's calling to observe the law of Moses. Only by following revealed truth can a person find God's wisdom.

1:11-30 What the fear of God offers

Having moved from intellectual wisdom (1:2-3) to practical wisdom as enshrined in the Torah (1:10), Ben Sira develops a picture of wise conduct, expressed as fear of God. This is not a craven submission, but a respectful reverence toward God (Prov 2:1-5). It also includes the idea of following one's conscience. On the basis of Deuteronomy 10:12 Ben Sira equates fearing God with loving him (2:15).

The poem begins with the assertion that the fear of the Lord means "glory and exultation" (1:11). All cultures have their own sense of honor, but this sense was acute in many parts of the Hellenistic world, including

¹⁹Knowledge and full understanding she rains down;
she heightens the glory of those who possess her.

²⁰The root of wisdom is to fear the Lord;
her branches are long life.
²¹The fear of the Lord drives away sins;
where it abides it turns back all anger.

◄ ²²Unjust anger can never be justified;
anger pulls a person to utter ruin.
²³Until the right time, the patient remain calm,
then cheerfulness comes back to them.
²⁴Until the right time they hold back their words;
then the lips of many will tell of their good sense.

²⁵Among wisdom's treasures is the model for knowledge;
but godliness is an abomination to the sinner.
²⁶If you desire wisdom, keep the commandments,
and the Lord will bestow her upon you;
²⁷For the fear of the Lord is wisdom and discipline;

---

the Palestine of Ben Sira's day. Elsewhere the sage insists that one gains honor not by military exploits but by obeying God's law (4:20-21; 42:2).

Ben Sira treats fear of God at the start of his book because the fear of the Lord is the beginning of wisdom (Ps 111:10; Prov 1:7; 9:10). While other good things in life may bring more immediate pleasures, the fear of the Lord gives lasting joy (40:26). The sage follows earlier biblical teaching (Prov 3:2; Deut 30:20) in promising a "long life" on earth to the God-fearer (1:12).

According to 1:14-21, the fear of the Lord is not only the beginning of wisdom but also wisdom's fullness and crown and root. Because wisdom is formed with the faithful in the womb, it belongs innately to the Israelites as their heritage (24:8), and hence Ben Sira's students do not need to seek Greek philosophy to gain true understanding. Rather, wisdom is the inheritance of the devout, such as those listed in the Praise of the Ancestors (44:1–50:24). Through fear of the Lord the believer will receive wisdom's rich harvest and the gift of health (6:19; 34:17-20), as the book of Proverbs already promises (Prov 3:7-8; 8:19). According to 1:20, wisdom's root grows up to produce branches (14:26; 24:16), equivalent to long life on this earth (Prov 3:2).

▶ This symbol indicates a cross-reference number in the *Catechism of the Catholic Church*. See page 152 for number citations.

faithfulness and humility are his
delight.

²⁸Do not disobey the fear of the Lord,
do not approach it with duplicity
of heart.
²⁹Do not be a hypocrite before others;
over your lips keep watch.
³⁰Do not exalt yourself lest you fall
and bring dishonor upon yourself;

For then the Lord will reveal your
secrets
and cast you down in the midst
of the assembly.
Because you did not approach the
fear of the Lord,
and your heart was full of deceit.

Trust in God

2 ¹My child, when you come to serve
the Lord,
prepare yourself for trials.
²Be sincere of heart and steadfast,
and do not be impetuous in time
of adversity.
³Cling to him, do not leave him,
that you may prosper in your
last days.

⁴Accept whatever happens to you;
in periods of humiliation be
patient.
⁵For in fire gold is tested,
and the chosen, in the crucible
of humiliation.
⁶Trust in God, and he will help you;

The statement that "the fear of the Lord turns back all anger" (1:21) com-
pletes 1:14-20 and provides a link to the mention of anger in 1:22. Because
human wrath does not accomplish God's righteousness (Prov 15:18; Jas
1:20), Ben Sira urges his students to control their anger. The self-controlled
person will receive public praise for being patient (Prov 14:29).

Sirach 1:25-27 links wisdom, the commandments, and fear of God (Prov
2:5-6; Deut 4:5-6; 10:12-13). The fear of the Lord entails "faithfulness and
humility," such as were shown by Moses (45:4). In 1:28-30 the sage recommends a sincere and reverent attitude toward God, because duplicity will
lead to embarrassment. Ben Sira cautions his students against the double
path of trying to remain faithful to Israel's God while accepting all the
values of the pagan Hellenistic culture. Seeking to gain status in this way
will lead to a disgraceful downfall (Prov 5:12-14; 16:18).

2:1-18 Be prepared for testing

After introducing the themes of wisdom and fear of God, the sage immediately warns that the way of God's wisdom can involve testing. This
motif occurs elsewhere in the Bible (Gen 22:1; Deut 8:2). In Ben Sira's view,
wisdom is acquired at the cost of trials, but in the end produces blessings
(4:17-18; 6:24-31).

The poem begins bluntly (2:1): the student is to be ready for trials (Acts
14:22). Already in the Jerusalem of Ben Sira's day, it was hard for the wor-

make your ways straight and
hope in him.

⁷You that fear the Lord, wait for his
mercy,
do not stray lest you fall.
⁸You that fear the Lord, trust in him,
and your reward will not be lost.

⁹You that fear the LORD, hope for
good things,
for lasting joy and mercy.

¹⁰Consider the generations long past
and see:
has anyone trusted in the Lord
and been disappointed?

---

shiper of Israel's God to resist the pressure to follow pagan Greek practices. This pressure increased after 175 B.C., following the accession of King Antiochus Epiphanes, who banned many practices of the Jewish religion (1 Macc 1:41-64). Christian readers might also recall Jesus' words about taking up the cross and following him (Mark 8:34). An illustration of 2:3-6 would be the story of Job's endurance of suffering (Job 1:1–2:10; Jas 5:11). The testing of human beings by trials can have a refining effect, as with gold in the furnace (Prov 17:3; Wis 3:6). Trust in God will be the prelude to divine help (Ps 37:3-6; Prov 3:5-6).

In 2:7-9 Ben Sira thrice urges his students to have faith and hope in God (1 Pet 1:21), so that like the redeemed Israelites they may have lasting joy (Isa 51:11). Sirach 2:10 uses three rhetorical questions to appeal to the past experience of the people of Israel (Deut 32:7). Ben Sira's confidence in divine help builds on the experience of the psalmist (Ps 34:8; 37:25). Even the sufferer who feels abandoned by God (Ps 22:2; Mark 15:34) will eventually be rescued (Ps 22:24-25; Acts 2:31-32). To be sure, Ben Sira's words of encouragement do not fully explain the mystery of suffering, as experienced by victims of genocide or famine, for instance. The sage boldly repeats the biblical proclamation that God is merciful, as first made to Moses (Exod 34:6) and often recalled since (Ps 111:4; Jas 5:11).

Ben Sira then launches into a threefold woe, addressed to the faithless (2:12-14). The fainthearted tread a double path by claiming to be members of the Israelite community yet also following pagan ways. Unlike the truly God-fearing (34:19), such faithless people will have nowhere to hide on the day of God's visitation (Wis 5:14-16). The devout person lovingly reverences God by humbly keeping the divine law and enduring trials (Deut 8:2; 10:12-13).

As a model for accepting suffering (2:18), Ben Sira alludes to David's choice to fall directly into God's hands by accepting a plague sent to punish Israel (2 Sam 24:14). Though God is great (18:5), God's mercy is just as great (Wis 11:21-23).

Has anyone persevered in his fear
and been forsaken?
has anyone called upon him and
been ignored?
¹¹For the Lord is compassionate and
merciful;
forgives sins and saves in time
of trouble.

¹²Woe to timid hearts and drooping
hands,
to the sinner who walks a double
path!
¹³Woe to the faint of heart! For they
do not trust,
and therefore have no shelter!
¹⁴Woe to you that have lost hope!
what will you do at the Lord's
visitation?

¹⁵Those who fear the Lord do not
disobey his words;
those who love him keep his
ways.
¹⁶Those who fear the Lord seek to
please him;

those who love him are filled
with his law.
¹⁷Those who fear the Lord prepare
their hearts
and humble themselves before
him.

¹⁸Let us fall into the hands of the Lord
and not into the hands of mortals,
For equal to his majesty is his mercy;
and equal to his name are his
works.

Responsibilities to Parents

3 ¹Children, listen to me, your father;
act accordingly, that you may be
safe.
²For the Lord sets a father in honor
over his children
and confirms a mother's
authority over her sons.
³Those who honor their father
atone for sins;
⁴they store up riches who respect
their mother.

3:1-16 Honor toward parents

Because wisdom involves obeying the divine law (1:26), Ben Sira urges his students to obey the precept to honor father and mother (Exod 20:12; Deut 5:16). The commandment covers not only young children's obedience to their adult parents, but also the respectful care shown by adults toward their aged parents (Mark 7:10-12). Ben Sira lived in a traditional society where respect was due to parents and older persons (7:27-28; 25:3-6).

Sirach 3:2-6 recalls the biblical promise that obedience to parents will lead to a long life (Exod 20:12; Deut 5:16). Like almsgiving, caring for one's father is a good work that brings atonement for one's sins (3:3, 30), just as care of one's mother is a sort of financial investment (Tob 4:8-9) for the future. Moreover, those who honor their father will receive the blessing of their own children (Ps 128:1-3), and God will hear their prayer because they have fulfilled their duty (Prov 15:29). God-fearing children will serve their parents like slaves (3:7), an exaggerated way of expressing the devotedness of the care (7:27-28).

⁵Those who honor their father will have joy in their own children,
and when they pray they are heard.
⁶Those who respect their father will live a long life;
those who obey the Lord honor their mother.

⁷Those who fear the Lord honor their father,
and serve their parents as masters.
⁸In word and deed honor your father,
that all blessings may come to you.
⁹A father's blessing gives a person firm roots,
but a mother's curse uproots the growing plant.
¹⁰Do not glory in your father's disgrace,
for that is no glory to you!
¹¹A father's glory is glory also for oneself;
they multiply sin who demean their mother.

¹²My son, be steadfast in honoring your father;
do not grieve him as long as he lives.
¹³Even if his mind fails, be considerate of him;
do not revile him because you are in your prime.
¹⁴Kindness to a father will not be forgotten;
it will serve as a sin offering—it will take lasting root.
¹⁵In time of trouble it will be recalled to your advantage,
like warmth upon frost it will melt away your sins.
¹⁶Those who neglect their father are like blasphemers;
those who provoke their mother are accursed by their Creator.

Humility

¹⁷My son, conduct your affairs with humility,
and you will be loved more than a giver of gifts.
¹⁸Humble yourself the more, the greater you are,

According to 3:8, those honoring their parents will be blessed for obeying the divine law (Deut 28:1-2). A blessing from parents can cause a family to take root and flourish (Prov 12:3). One is not to take pleasure in the disgraceful condition of a parent (3:10-11), because the glory of children is their parents (Prov 17:6). Indeed, cursing one's parents is self-destructive (Prov 20:20). Hence 3:12-16 urges proper filial care of senile parents, who deserve respect even in their infirmity (Prov 23:22; Tob 4:3). Kindness to aged parents counterbalances one's earlier sins, whereas despising parents is an offense against God (Prov 19:26; 30:17).

3:17-29 A humble attitude

While Moses was praised for his meekness (Num 12:3) and Proverbs inculcates a modest attitude (Prov 11:2; 15:33), Ben Sira makes humility one

and you will find mercy in the sight of God.
²⁰For great is the power of the Lord; by the humble he is glorified.
²¹What is too sublime for you, do not seek; do not reach into things that are hidden from you.
²²What is committed to you, pay heed to; what is hidden is not your concern.
²³In matters that are beyond you do not meddle, when you have been shown more than you can understand.
²⁴Indeed, many are the conceits of human beings; evil imaginations lead them astray.

Docility
²⁵Without the pupil of the eye, light is missing; without knowledge, wisdom is missing.
²⁶A stubborn heart will fare badly in the end; those who love danger will perish in it.
²⁷A stubborn heart will have many a hurt; adding sin to sin is madness.
²⁸When the proud are afflicted, there is no cure; for they are offshoots of an evil plant.
²⁹The mind of the wise appreciates proverbs, and the ear that listens to wisdom rejoices.

of his special hallmarks (1:27; 7:17), thereby anticipating Jesus' way of humility (Matt 18:1-4).

Sirach 3:17 urges the student to walk humbly (Mic 6:8), since paradoxically humility will lead to honor (Luke 14:11). The greater the humility that is shown, the more the favor that will be received from God. Ben Sira reminds readers that God's power is great, far beyond the power of any human being (18:5). God is glorified by the humble, because they know their own weakness (2 Cor 12:9). Some late manuscripts add a comment in 3:19.

Ben Sira's counsel (3:21-24) to avoid setting one's sights too high draws on Psalm 131:1. In the original context, the marvels beyond human knowledge may refer both to apocalyptic revelations and to the wonders of Greek science. Rather than attending to matters too great, students are invited to pay attention to what has been shown to them, namely, God's law (Deut 29:28).

Just as the eye needs to be open to receive light (3:25), so the mind must be open to receive wisdom (Luke 11:34-36). The person who stubbornly risks danger will come to a bad end (Prov 28:14). As in Wisdom 12:10, Ben Sira regards the arrogant person as the offshoot of an evil plant (40:15-16).

Alms for the Poor

³⁰As water quenches a flaming fire,
so almsgiving atones for sins.
³¹The kindness people have done
crosses their paths later on;
should they stumble, they will
find support.

4 ¹My child, do not mock the life of
the poor;
do not keep needy eyes waiting.
²Do not grieve the hungry,
nor anger the needy.
³Do not aggravate a heart already
angry,
nor delay giving to the needy.
⁴A beggar's request do not reject;
do not turn your face away from
the poor.
⁵From the needy do not turn your
eyes;
do not give them reason to curse
you.
⁶If in their pain they cry out
bitterly,
their Rock will hear the sound
of their cry.

Social Conduct

⁷Endear yourself to the assembly;
before the city's ruler bow your
head.
⁸Give a hearing to the poor,
and return their greeting with
deference;
⁹Deliver the oppressed from their
oppressors;
right judgment should not be
repugnant to you.
¹⁰Be like a father to orphans,
and take the place of a husband
to widows.

3:30–4:10 Principles of social justice

The opening point that almsgiving can atone for sin occurs elsewhere in the Bible (Dan 4:24; Tob 12:9). According to Ben Sira (7:1; 27:26-27), kindness produces its own reward, but evil recoils on the head of its practitioners (Tob 14:10-11; Prov 26:27). In fact, the sage holds the traditional Israelite view that good deeds are rewarded and evil deeds punished (Deut 28:1-68; Prov 11:8).

In 4:3 Ben Sira urges his students not to delay their giving to the needy (Prov 3:28), because those who attend to the plea of the poor will be like God (Ps 22:25; Tob 4:7). The one who ignores the needs of the destitute will become the victim of their curse (Exod 22:21-23; Prov 28:27), whereas the helper of the poor will receive their blessing (Job 31:20). Since one Maker created rich and poor (Prov 22:2; Job 31:15), all persons deserve respect (Prov 14:31).

According to 4:9, those who achieve positions of responsibility are to use their power to rescue the oppressed (Ps 82:2-4; Prov 31:8-9). If the Most High is "father of the fatherless, defender of widows" (Ps 68:6), one becomes like God by assisting these persons in their need (Job 29:16). Thereby a person becomes a true child of God (Ps 82:6; Luke 6:35). Whereas the He-

Then God will call you his child,
and he will be merciful to you and
deliver you from the pit.

The Rewards of Wisdom

¹¹Wisdom teaches her children
and admonishes all who can
understand her.
¹²Those who love her love life;
those who seek her out win the
Lord's favor.
¹³Those who hold her fast will attain
glory,
and they shall abide in the blessing of the Lord.
¹⁴Those who serve her serve the
Holy One;
those who love her the Lord loves.
¹⁵"Whoever obeys me will judge
nations;
whoever listens to me will dwell
in my inmost chambers.
¹⁶If they remain faithful, they will
possess me;
their descendants too will inherit
me.
¹⁷"I will walk with them in disguise,
and at first I will test them with
trials.
Fear and dread I will bring upon
them
and I will discipline them with
my constraints.

brew text speaks of God delivering a generous person from death (Tob 14:10-11), the Greek version of 4:10d employs maternal imagery for God: "He will love you more than your mother does" (cf. Isa 49:15; 66:13).

USING WISDOM PERSONALLY

Sirach 4:11–6:17

4:11-19 Learning wisdom

The poem opening the second section of Ben Sira's book presents the rewards of wisdom while also acknowledging the hardships involved in acquiring it. Ben Sira calls the recipients of personified wisdom "her children" (Luke 7:35).

Wisdom's basic reward is "life" (4:12), as in Proverbs 8:35. Ben Sira echoes the choice between life and death that Moses placed before the Israelites (Deut 30:15). The point of 4:12 is not only that the wise person will avoid dangerous situations (3:26; 9:13), but also that wisdom itself is a source of life (Prov 3:18). In 4:14 the sage seems to liken wisdom's servants to those serving God's sanctuary in the Jerusalem temple (24:10). According to 4:15, one who understands wisdom will judge nations (Wis 3:8; 1 Cor 6:2).

Ben Sira develops the female personification of wisdom in 4:17-19. The hardships of wisdom begin with the difficult task of going around with her while she seems a stranger. Then she will probe the student with trials,

When their hearts are fully with me,
^{18}then I will set them again on
the straight path
and reveal my secrets to them.
^{19}But if they turn away from me,
I will abandon them
and deliver them over to robbers."

Sincerity and Justice

^{20}My son, watch for the right time;
fear what is evil;
do not bring shame upon yourself.
^{21}There is a shame heavy with guilt,
and a shame that brings glory
and respect.
^{22}Show no favoritism to your own
discredit;
let no one intimidate you to your
own downfall.
^{23}Do not refrain from speaking at
the proper time,
and do not hide your wisdom;
^{24}For wisdom becomes known
through speech,

and knowledge through the
tongue's response.
^{25}Never speak against the truth,
but of your own ignorance be
ashamed.
^{26}Do not be ashamed to acknowledge your sins,
and do not struggle against a
rushing stream.
^{27}Do not abase yourself before a fool;
do not refuse to do so before
rulers.
^{28}Even to the death, fight for what is
right,
and the Lord will do battle for
you.

^{29}Do not be haughty in your speech,
or lazy and slack in your deeds.
^{30}Do not be like a lion at home,
or sly and suspicious with your
servants.
^{31}Do not let your hand be open to
receive,
but clenched when it is time to
give.

---

making the learner choose between wise and foolish actions. But eventually, when the learner's heart is filled with wisdom, she will reveal her secrets.

4:20-31 Honesty

By keeping from evildoing, a person will avoid shame, the disgrace dreaded by people in the Hellenistic world (5:13–6:1; 41:16–42:8). Sirach 4:21 distinguishes a wrongful shame (dependent on the opinions of others and leading to sin) from a modest shame (a careful avoidance of sin which in fact leads to honor). In 4:23 Ben Sira insists that a false sense of shame should not hold people back from uttering their wisdom at the right moment (20:30-31).

Because truth is like an unstoppable stream (4:25-26), it is pointless to cover up one's sinfulness. There is no disgrace in acknowledging guilt, though ignorant folly is a cause for real shame. The sage's admonition to fight for what is right, even to the point of death (4:28), was heeded a few

Against Presumption

5 ¹Do not rely on your wealth,
   or say, "I have the power."
²Do not rely on your strength
   in following the desires of your
   heart.
³Do not say, "Who can prevail
   against me?"
   for the LORD will exact punishment.
⁴Do not say, "I have sinned, yet
   what has happened to me?"
   for the LORD is slow to anger!
⁵Do not be so confident of forgiveness
   that you add sin upon sin.
⁶Do not say, "His mercy is great;
   my many sins he will forgive."
For mercy and anger alike are with
   him;
   his wrath comes to rest on the
   wicked.

⁷Do not delay turning back to the
   LORD,
   do not put it off day after day.
For suddenly his wrath will come
   forth;
   at the time of vengeance, you
   will perish.
⁸Do not rely on deceitful wealth,
   for it will be no help on the day
   of wrath.

Use and Abuse of the Tongue

⁹Do not winnow in every wind,
   nor walk in every path.
¹⁰Be steadfast regarding your
   knowledge,
   and let your speech be consistent.
¹¹Be swift to hear,
   but slow to answer.
¹²If you can, answer your neighbor;
   if not, place your hand over your
   mouth!

---

years later by the Maccabean martyrs (2 Macc 6:18-20; 7:1-2). Sirach 4:31 commends giving rather than receiving (Acts 20:35).

5:1–6:4 Against presumption and insincerity

Sirach 5:1-3 warns against arrogant self-sufficiency. Dependence on wealth is insecure (Luke 12:15; 1 Tim 6:17), while human desires can lead a person astray. In 5:3 the sage urges a humble recognition that God is more powerful than we are (1 Cor 10:22).

It is wrong to boast if no punishment has followed one's sin (5:4), because God can show wrath as well as mercy toward humanity (16:11). Indeed, sinners are regarded as deserving divine anger (Rom 1:18). Hence the sage solemnly warns against postponing repentance, lest one suddenly become a victim of God's displeasure (5:7). Moreover, wealth gained by unjust means will be useless if God decides to bring punishment (Prov 10:2).

Using images from agriculture and travel, 5:9 advocates sincere and consistent speech. Common sense entails being quick to hear and slow to respond (5:11), an insight that the letter of James borrows from Ben Sira (Jas 1:19). Sirach 5:12 employs graphic imagery to inculcate silence when one has nothing sensible to say. Speech may bring honor or dishonor, and the

¹³Honor and dishonor through
    speaking!
The tongue can be your downfall.
¹⁴Do not be called double-tongued;
    and with your tongue do not
        slander a neighbor.
For shame has been created for the
    thief,
    and sore disgrace for the double-
        tongued.
¹⁵In little or in much, do not act
    corruptly;

6 ¹Do not be a foe instead of a friend.
    A bad name, disgrace, and dis-
        honor you will inherit.
    Thus the wicked, the double-
        tongued!

Unruly Passions

²Do not fall into the grip of your
    passion,
    lest like fire it consume your
        strength.

³It will eat your leaves and destroy
    your fruits,
    and you will be left like a dry
        tree.
⁴For fierce passion destroys its
    owner
    and makes him the sport of his
        enemies.

True Friendship

⁵Pleasant speech multiplies friends,
    and gracious lips, friendly greet-
        ings.
⁶Let those who are friendly to you
    be many,
    but one in a thousand your
        confidant.
⁷When you gain friends, gain them
    through testing,
    and do not be quick to trust
        them.
⁸For there are friends when it suits
    them,

---

tongue can be a person's downfall (Prov 18:21). Like thieves, the double-tongued deserve disgrace (Prov 18:7).

The final passage (6:2-4) warns of the danger of lustful desire which, if not controlled, can overwhelm someone. Sirach 6:3 compares such a person with a tree (Jer 17:5-6) destroyed by fire. Unrestrained desire can make people the laughing stock of their enemies.

6:5-17 The value of true friendship

Ben Sira has much to say on friendship (9:10-16; 22:19-26; 27:16-21; 37:1-6). While the book of Proverbs includes scattered sayings on the topic (Prov 17:17; 19:4-7; 27:10), Ben Sira collects his thoughts into longer passages.

Polite speech is a prerequisite of friendship (6:5), since a rude response will spoil any chance of making friends (Prov 16:21; 22:11). Yet though everyone deserves a polite greeting, few deserve to be trusted. Rather than trusting a person instantly, one should test the genuineness of the friendship (Matt 7:16), particularly by evaluating the friend's behavior in one's adversity.

but they will not be around in
time of trouble.
⁹Another is a friend who turns into
an enemy,
and tells of the quarrel to your
disgrace.
¹⁰Others are friends, table companions,
but they cannot be found in time
of affliction.
¹¹When things go well, they are your
other self,
and lord it over your servants.
¹²If disaster comes upon you, they
turn against you
and hide themselves.
¹³Stay away from your enemies,
and be on guard with your
friends.
¹⁴Faithful friends are a sturdy shelter;
whoever finds one finds a treasure.

¹⁵Faithful friends are beyond price,
no amount can balance their
worth.
¹⁶Faithful friends are life-saving
medicine;
those who fear God will find
them.
¹⁷Those who fear the Lord enjoy
stable friendship,
for as they are, so will their
neighbors be.

Blessings of Wisdom
¹⁸My child, from your youth choose
discipline;
and when you have gray hair
you will find wisdom.
¹⁹As though plowing and sowing,
draw close to her;
then wait for her bountiful crops.
For in cultivating her you will work
but little,

The need for testing a potential friend is elaborated in 6:8-13. The sage's caution is based on the unreliability of fair-weather friends, who are happy to be table partners, but who run away at a time of need and even disclose confidences. Apparently Ben Sira had been betrayed by his former friends, and had been saved only with God's help (51:2-3). Hence, besides keeping away from enemies (as expected), one should also (unexpectedly) be on guard in dealings with friends.

After the negative tone of 6:8-13, the sage describes the loyal friend (6:14-17). The image of "sturdy shelter" suggests a good friend's protective quality. Such a person is a priceless treasure; in 26:15 the sage uses similar language for the chaste wife. Sirach 6:16 states that the God-fearing person will find such loyal friends, because like is attracted to like (13:15-16).

APPLYING WISDOM SOCIALLY

Sirach 6:18–14:19

6:18-37 Wisdom's blessings

The book's third part opens with a poem on the hardships and benefits of gaining wisdom. Students need to acquire wisdom in their youth through

and soon you will eat her
fruit.

²⁰She is rough ground to the fool!
The stupid cannot abide her.
²¹She will be like a burdensome
stone to them,
and they will not delay in casting
her aside.
²²For discipline is like her name,
she is not accessible to many.

²³Listen, my child, and take my
advice;
do not refuse my counsel.
²⁴Put your feet into her fetters,
and your neck under her yoke.
²⁵Bend your shoulders and carry her
and do not be irked at her bonds.

²⁶With all your soul draw close to her;
and with all your strength keep
her ways.
²⁷Inquire and search, seek and find;
when you get hold of her, do not
let her go.
²⁸Thus at last you will find rest in her,
and she will become your joy.

²⁹Her fetters will be a place of
strength;
her snare, a robe of spun gold.
³⁰Her yoke will be a gold ornament;
her bonds, a purple cord.
³¹You will wear her as a robe of
glory,
and bear her as a splendid crown.

³²If you wish, my son, you can be
wise;
if you apply yourself, you can be
shrewd.
³³If you are willing to listen, you can
learn;
if you pay attention, you can be
instructed.

³⁴Stand in the company of the
elders;
stay close to whoever is wise.
³⁵Be eager to hear every discourse;
let no insightful saying escape
you.
³⁶If you see the intelligent, seek them
out;
let your feet wear away their
doorsteps!

---

a disciplined approach to life (25:3; 31:22). Sirach 6:19 uses the imagery of sowing and reaping (2 Cor 9:6; Gal 6:7-9). A rich harvest results from the effort given to acquiring wisdom, though the fool regards discipline as a heavy burden to be cast aside. As the sage notes elsewhere (2:4-5; 4:17), the hardship of discipline is self-evident (Prov 12:1; Heb 12:11).

Sirach 6:24-25 compares this wise discipline to a yoke and fetters. Later rabbis spoke of the yoke of the law of Moses (*Mishnah Aboth* 3.5), while Jesus invites his followers to take his yoke upon themselves (Matt 11:29). The quest for wisdom is to be undertaken with one's whole soul and strength, like loving God (Deut 6:5). To find wisdom, a person must first seek it (Matt 7:7). Once found, wisdom should be held firmly (Prov 4:13), because it will eventually provide contentment (15:6).

Though discipline seems like fetters and bonds for a fool (6:29-30), it represents a glorious garment for the sensible person (21:19, 21). According to Numbers 15:38-40, the Israelites were to use a purple cord to tie tassels

³⁷Reflect on the law of the Most High,
  and let his commandments be
    your constant study.
Then he will enlighten your mind,
  and make you wise as you
    desire.

Conduct Toward God and Neighbor

7 ¹Do no evil, and evil will not over-
    take you;
  ²avoid wickedness, and it will
    turn away from you.
³Do not sow in the furrows of injus-
    tice,
  lest you harvest it sevenfold.

⁴Do not seek from God authority
  or from the king a place of
    honor.
⁵Do not parade your righteousness
    before the LORD,
  and before the king do not flaunt
    your wisdom.
⁶Do not seek to become a judge
  if you do not have the strength
    to root out crime,
Lest you show fear in the presence
    of the prominent
  and mar your integrity.
⁷Do not be guilty of any evil before
    the city court

---

to the corner of their garments, as a visual reminder of all God's commands; Ben Sira sees wisdom as having a similar function. Indeed wisdom will provide the student with a glorious robe such as the high priest wore (50:11), as well as a splendid crown (Prov 4:9).

In 6:32-33 the sage invites the student to choose to become wise (15:15-17). Wisdom can be acquired by associating with sensible persons (8:8-9; 9:14-16). This biblical teaching (Prov 13:20) is matched by an Egyptian wisdom saying: "The friend of a fool is a fool; the friend of a wise person is a wise person" (*Ankhsheshonq* 13.6). The sensible student will also gain wisdom by reflecting on God's commands revealed in the Scriptures (1:26; 19:20).

7:1-17 Conduct in public life

The next poem outlines the practical implications of the wisdom commended in 6:18-37, in terms of upright and humble behavior in one's social life. The first verse (often quoted by the rabbis) reminds us that much of the evil we suffer comes to us from our own evildoing (Num 32:23). For instance, 2 Samuel traces David's family problems back to his adultery with Bathsheba (2 Sam 12:9-12). Using an agricultural metaphor, the sage warns against sowing injustice, since the harvest will be seven times worse (Job 4:8; Gal 6:8).

Since Ben Sira's students were young men from the upper classes, in 7:4-7 he warns them against ambition (Prov 25:6-7; Luke 14:8). It is unwise to claim to be upright before God, because everybody sins (Ps 143:2; Rom 3:9-10). Likewise, it is foolish to flaunt one's wisdom before the king, whose intentions may be unfathomable (Prov 25:3). A judge has the weighty

or disgrace yourself before the assembly.
⁸Do not plot to repeat a sin;
even for one, you will not go unpunished.
⁹Do not say, "He will appreciate my many gifts;
the Most High God will accept my offerings."
¹⁰Do not be impatient in prayer
or neglect almsgiving.
¹¹Do not ridicule the embittered;
Remember: there is One who exalts and humbles.
¹²Do not plot mischief against your relative
or against your friend and companion.
¹³Refuse to tell lie after lie,
for it never results in good.
¹⁴Do not babble in the assembly of the elders
or repeat the words of your prayer.
¹⁵Do not hate hard work;
work was assigned by God.
¹⁶Do not esteem yourself more than your compatriots;
remember, his wrath will not delay.
¹⁷More and more, humble your pride;
what awaits mortals is worms.

---

responsibility to root out crime by withstanding the forces of evil (Lev 19:15), but disgrace results from yielding to unjust pressure from the powerful. For the sage, public shaming is a strong sanction against sin (1:30). Sirach 7:8-10 warns that proud sin is inevitably punished, and a multitude of offerings to God cannot be a substitute for upright behavior (Amos 5:21-24; Isa 1:11-15).

In 7:11-17 the sage again counsels upright and humble conduct. Mocking the unfortunate is stupid, since the God who raised you up and brought the other person down can reverse the balance (11:4-6). According to 7:13, lies produce evil results (Hos 10:13). Thoughtless words are inappropriate whether in a political meeting or in prayer. Moreover, physical work was allotted to humanity by God (Gen 2:15; 3:19) and thus has its own dignity (38:24-34). The rabbis taught that Torah study should be combined with manual labor (*Mishnah Aboth* 2.2).

An incentive to humility is the realization that what awaits humanity after death is bodily decay (Job 25:6). In line with earlier biblical texts (Isa 38:18; Job 14:7-12), Ben Sira has no belief in an afterlife. However, whereas the Hebrew text asserts that "what awaits mortals is worms," the grandson's Greek version of 7:17b introduces the idea of penalties after death: "The punishment of the impious is fire and worms," using imagery as in other biblical books (Isa 66:24; Jdt 16:17; Mark 9:47-48). By the time the grandson made the Greek translation, the idea of rewards and punishments after death had become more widely accepted among the Jews (Dan 12:2-3; 2 Macc 7:14).

Duties of Family Life, Religion and Charity

¹⁸Do not barter a friend for money,
   or a true brother for the gold of
      Ophir.
¹⁹Do not reject a sensible wife;
   a gracious wife is more precious
      than pearls.
²⁰Do not mistreat a servant who
      works faithfully,
   or laborers who devote them-
      selves to their task.
²¹Love wise servants as yourself;
   do not refuse them freedom.
²²Do you have livestock? Look after
      them;
   if they are dependable, keep them.
²³Do you have sons? Correct them
   and cure their stubbornness in
      their early youth.
²⁴Do you have daughters? Keep them
      chaste,
   and do not be indulgent to them.
²⁵Give your daughter in marriage,
   and a worry comes to an end;
   but give her to a sensible man.
²⁶Do you have a wife? Do not mis-
      treat her,
   but do not trust the wife you hate.

7:18-36 Duties toward others

Ben Sira next spells out duties toward members of society: family, friends, the priests, and the needy. Since friends are "beyond price" (6:15), one should not barter them for money. Ophir (perhaps in Arabia) was proverbial as a source of fine gold (1 Kgs 9:28; Job 28:16). Ben Sira praises a sensible and gracious wife, who is more precious than pearls (Prov 31:10).

Sirach 7:20-21 counsels fair treatment of a faithful household servant (33:31-33) and of a laborer (Deut 24:14). A wise servant is to be loved as oneself (Lev 19:18), and should be offered freedom in the seventh year as the Torah commands (Exod 21:2; Deut 15:12). As in many African countries today, cattle can be a source of wealth for people in the Near East (Gen 13:2), and so these valuable animals deserve to be looked after (Prov 27:23-27).

Rearing of sons involves disciplining them (Prov 13:24) and submitting their neck to the yoke of obedience (30:12-13). However, 7:23b in the Hebrew says: "Choose wives for them in their youth," referring to the Jewish tradition that a father should provide a wife for his son before he is too old (tractate *Qiddushin* 30b in the Babylonian Talmud). In a traditional patriarchal society, rearing of daughters involved guarding their chastity (42:9-10). Marrying off a daughter meant getting rid of a source of worry for a father, provided she married a wise husband. In 7:26 Ben Sira urges faithful love of one's wife in normal circumstances, but distrust of her if she is hated, perhaps meaning divorced. The law of Moses made provision for divorce (Deut 24:1-4), though Jesus forbade it (Mark 10:9).

Sirach 7:27-31 alludes to the *Shema* (Deut 6:5), with its command to love God with all one's heart and soul and strength. For Ben Sira, this precept

◄ ²⁷With your whole heart honor your
father;
your mother's birth pangs do
not forget.
²⁸Remember, of these parents you
were born;
what can you give them for all
they gave you?

²⁹With all your soul fear God
and revere his priests.
³⁰With all your strength love your
Maker
and do not neglect his ministers.
³¹Honor God and respect the priest;
give him his portion as you have
been commanded:
First fruits and contributions,
his portion of victims and holy
offerings.

³²To the poor also extend your hand,
that your blessing may be complete.
³³Give your gift to all the living,
and do not withhold your kindness from the dead.
³⁴Do not avoid those who weep,
but mourn with those who mourn.
³⁵Do not hesitate to visit the sick,
because for such things you will
be loved.

³⁶In whatever you do, remember
your last days,
and you will never sin.

Prudence in Dealing with Others

8 ¹Do not contend with the mighty,
lest you fall into their power.
²Do not quarrel with the rich,

---

includes love of parents and respect for the temple priesthood. While the
command to honor and care for father and mother is included in the Ten
Commandments (Exod 20:12; Deut 5:16), the sage emphasizes the motive
of gratitude (Tob 4:3-4). Respect for God also involves revering the Aaronic
priests as holy (Lev 21:8), and love of the Creator includes attending to the
needs of God's ministers (Deut 12:19). Ben Sira urges his students to contribute the prescribed offerings to support the priests (Prov 3:9-10; Num
18:9-20).

Kindness to the poor (7:32) will be rewarded with the divine blessing
(Deut 14:28-29; Tob 4:7). Indeed, it is good to be generous to everyone, and
even contribute to burying the dead (Tob 1:17). Moreover, Ben Sira urges
his students to share the grief of mourners and visit the sick (Rom 12:15;
Matt 25:39-40). Finally, awareness of personal mortality will keep one
humble (7:17; 28:6), with a healthy reverence for God and respect for one's
neighbor.

8:1-19 Prudence in dealing with others

Sirach 8:1 warns against quarreling with influential persons, who might
become hostile. Upsetting the rich could lead them to bribe the ruling
powers against one (Prov 17:23). Arguing with a loud-mouthed person
(Prov 26:20-21) only adds fuel to the fire (28:8-11).

lest they pay out the price of
your downfall.
For gold has unsettled many,
and wealth perverts the character
of princes.

³Do not quarrel with loud-mouths,
or heap wood upon their fire.
⁴Do not associate with the senseless,
lest your ancestors be insulted.

⁵Do not reproach one who turns
away from sin;
remember, we all are guilty.
⁶Do not insult one who is old,
for some of us will also grow old.
⁷Do not rejoice when someone dies;
remember, we are all to be
gathered in.

⁸Do not neglect the discourse of the
wise,
but busy yourself with their
proverbs;
For in this way you will acquire the
training
to stand in the presence of princes.
⁹Do not reject the tradition of the
elders
which they have heard from
their ancestors;
For from it you will learn
how to answer when the need
arises.

¹⁰Do not kindle the coals of sinners,
lest you be burned in their flaming fire.

Sirach 8:5-7 advocates a sympathetic understanding toward human weakness. All human beings need to repent (17:24-25), because everyone sins (1 Kgs 8:46; Eccl 7:20). A society that despises the elderly despises its own future. To express the idea of death, Sirach 8:7b echoes the biblical expression "to be gathered" to one's ancestors (Gen 25:8; Judg 2:10).

In 8:8-9 Ben Sira urges openness to learning from older and wiser persons (Lev 19:32). Ancient Hebrew society respected the wisdom of the elders, who were regarded as possessing insight gained from their life experience and their knowledge of tradition (25:4-6). A willingness to learn from the wise (9:14-15; 39:1-4) will enable the sensible student to advance in society (Prov 22:29). The valuable ability to give an appropriate answer will come from listening to the spoken tradition of the elders (Prov 22:21).

Sirach 8:10-19 describes persons to be approached with caution. According to Ben Sira (28:10-11), a sinner's anger is easily kindled, with disastrous results (Prov 26:21). Lending to someone more powerful can mean saying goodbye to one's money (29:4-7), just as guaranteeing the loan of an influential person (29:16-19) can necessitate repaying it oneself (Prov 22:26-27). In the nature of things, it is impossible to win a case against a judge. Moreover, traveling with someone ruthless or angry will lead to harm. Sirach 8:17-18 warns against revealing a secret to a fool (who may pass it on to others) or to a stranger (who may misuse it). Indeed, any confiding in others may spoil one's happiness or prosperity.

¹¹Do not give ground before scoundrels;
  it will set them in ambush against you.
¹²Do not lend to one more powerful than yourself;
  or if you lend, count it as lost.
¹³Do not give collateral beyond your means;
  consider any collateral a debt you must pay.

¹⁴Do not go to court against a judge,
  for the case will be settled in his favor.
¹⁵Do not travel with the ruthless
  lest they weigh you down with calamity;
For they will only go their own way,
  and through their folly you will also perish.
¹⁶Do not defy the quick-tempered,
  or ride with them through the desert.
For bloodshed is nothing to them;
  when there is no one to help, they will destroy you.

¹⁷Do not take counsel with simpletons,
  for they cannot keep a confidence.
¹⁸Before a stranger do nothing that should be kept secret,
  for you do not know what it will produce later on.
¹⁹Open your heart to no one,
  do not banish your happiness.

Advice Concerning Women

9 ¹Do not be jealous of the wife of your bosom,
  lest you teach her to do evil against you.
²Do not give a woman power over you

9:1-9 Caution in relating to women

This is the first of several passages in which Ben Sira advises his students on relations with women (25:13–26:18; 42:9-14). The general attitude is cautious and even suspicious. As a teacher in a patriarchal society governed by rules of honor and shame, he warns his young male pupils of the moral danger of associating with loose women.

The sage begins by emphasizing respect for marriage. The young man is to avoid jealousy toward his wife, else she may be provoked to evil. In 9:2 Ben Sira displays his cautious outlook (33:20): giving power to a woman could enable her to disgrace her husband by trampling on his dignity (Prov 31:3). Moreover, the male student should avoid intimacy with a strange (or foreign) woman, who might catch him in her snares (Prov 7:23).

Sirach 9:5 advises against lustful thoughts toward a virgin (Job 31:1; Matt 5:28). Moreover, the student associating too closely with a married woman will go down in blood to the grave (Prov 2:18; 7:27), probably a reference to the death penalty stipulated for adulterers (Lev 20:10) or to the husband's revenge (Prov 6:34).

to trample on your dignity.
³Do not go near a strange woman,
lest you fall into her snares.
⁴Do not dally with a singer,
lest you be captivated by her
charms.
⁵Do not entertain any thoughts
about a virgin,
lest you be enmeshed in damages
for her.
⁶Do not give yourself to a prostitute
lest you lose your inheritance.
⁷Do not look around the streets of
the city
or wander through its squares.
⁸Avert your eyes from a shapely
woman;
do not gaze upon beauty that is
not yours;
Through woman's beauty many
have been ruined,
for love of it burns like fire.
⁹Never recline at table with a married
woman,
or drink intoxicants with her,

Lest your heart be drawn to her
and you go down in blood to
the grave.

Choice of Friends
¹⁰Do not abandon old friends;
new ones cannot equal them.
A new friend is like new wine—
when it has aged, you drink it
with pleasure.
¹¹Do not envy the wicked
for you do not know when their
day will come.
¹²Do not delight in the pleasures of
the ungodly;
remember, they will not die unpunished.

¹³Keep away from those who have
power to kill,
and you will not be filled with
the dread of death.
But if you come near them, do not
offend them,
lest they take away your life.

9:10-16 Caution in relating to men

An old mature friendship cannot easily be replaced by a new one (Luke 5:39); fidelity in friendship is important (6:14-16). The sage urges his students to distance themselves from sinners and the proud, who will receive retribution in this life (11:24-28). Moreover, Ben Sira's pupils will do well to keep away from the ruling power if they want to avoid the danger of death.

Instead, the students are encouraged to associate with truly wise persons (9:14-16), namely, those who are righteous and God-fearing (Prov 13:20). The Greek writer Xenophon (d. ca. 354 B.C.) makes a comparable assertion: "The society of honest persons is a training in virtue, but the society of the bad is virtue's undoing" (*Memorabilia* 1.2.20). In 9:16 Ben Sira appeals to his students to dine only with upright people. According to one of the Dead Sea Scrolls, it is the virtuous who know the divine wisdom: "Her voice is heard in the gates of the just; their meditation is on the law of the Most High" (11Q5 18.12-14).

Know that you are stepping among
      snares
   and walking over a net.

¹⁴As best you can, answer your
      neighbor,
   and associate with the wise.
¹⁵With the learned exchange ideas;
   and let all your conversation be
         about the law of the Most
         High.
¹⁶Take the righteous for your table
      companions;
   and let your glory be in the fear
      of God.

Concerning Rulers

¹⁷Work by skilled hands will earn
      praise;
   but the people's leader is proved
      wise by his words.
¹⁸Loud mouths are feared in their
      city,
   and whoever is reckless in
      speech is hated.

10 ¹A wise magistrate gives stability
      to his people,
   and government by the intelli-
      gent is well ordered.
²As the people's judge, so the offi-
      cials;
   as the head of a city, so the
      inhabitants.
³A reckless king destroys his people,
   but a city grows through the
      intelligence of its princes.
⁴Sovereignty over the earth is in the
      hand of God,
   who appoints the right person
      for the right time.
⁵Sovereignty over everyone is in the
      hand of God,
   who imparts his majesty to the
      ruler.

The Sin of Pride

⁶No matter what the wrong, never
      harm your neighbor
   or go the way of arrogance.

9:17–10:18 True greatness

The next section treats genuine greatness in two parts: on rulers (9:17–10:5) and on the sin of pride (10:6-18). Ben Sira first contrasts the skilled manual worker with the learned sage (38:24–39:11). Sirach 10:2 draws a parallel between ruler and ruled; either the people imitate their leader, or they get the government they deserve! According to 10:4-5, God is sovereign over all earthly rulers, and can grant them success or failure (10:14; 11:5-6).

In 10:6 the sage urges a humble response to a neighbor's evil action; here he anticipates the Sermon on the Mount (Matt 5:39). Since God hates arrogance, proud nations end by receiving divine retribution. Sirach 10:9-10 mocks human pride with a vivid proverb: "A king today—tomorrow he is dead." Then the human corpse becomes food for worms (7:17). According to 10:12-13, pride and sin are linked, leading to ruin (Gen 6:5-8). Hence, God dethrones the proud and raises the lowly (1 Sam 2:7-8; Luke 1:52). In the imagery of 10:15, God's destruction of the proud is like uprooting (Ps 52:7; Prov 2:22).

⁷Odious to the Lord and to mortals
      is pride,
   and for both oppression is a crime.
⁸Sovereignty is transferred from one
      people to another
   because of the lawlessness of the
      proud.
⁹Why are dust and ashes proud?
   Even during life the body decays.
¹⁰A slight illness—the doctor jests;
   a king today—tomorrow he is
      dead.
¹¹When a people die,
   they inherit corruption and
      worms, gnats and
      maggots.

¹²The beginning of pride is stub-
      bornness
   in withdrawing the heart from
      one's Maker.
¹³For sin is a reservoir of insolence,
   a source which runs over with
      vice;
Because of it God sends unheard-of
   afflictions
   and strikes people with utter
      ruin.
¹⁴God overturns the thrones of the
      proud
   and enthrones the lowly in their
      place.

¹⁵God plucks up the roots of the
      proud,
   and plants the lowly in their
      place.
¹⁶The Lord lays waste the lands of
      the nations,
   and destroys them to the very
      foundations of the earth.
¹⁷He removes them from the earth,
      destroying them,
   erasing their memory from the
      world.
¹⁸Insolence does not befit mortals,
   nor impudent anger those born
      of women.

True Glory

¹⁹Whose offspring can be honorable?
      Human offspring.
   Those who fear the LORD are
      honorable offspring.
   Whose offspring can be disgraceful?
      Human offspring.
   Those who transgress the com-
      mandment are disgraceful
      offspring.
²⁰Among relatives their leader is
      honored;
   but whoever fears God is honored
      among God's people.
²²Resident alien, stranger, foreigner,
      pauper—

10:19–11:6 True glory

This finely crafted poem comments on the rise and fall of human beings. The powerful receive honor but may fall through foolish pride, whereas the powerless are often despised yet may rise through humble wisdom. According to 10:19, true honor comes not from status or wealth but from fear of God (Jer 9:22-23). Hence, honor is due to a wise pauper rather than a lawless person (Jas 2:1-4). Though civil rulers deserve appropriate respect, the greatest honor belongs to a God-fearing person. Indeed, a prudent slave may rise to have power over free persons (Prov 17:2). A well-fed laborer is better than a hungry boaster (Prov 12:9), because there is no shame in honest work (7:15).

their glory is the fear of the LORD.
²³It is not right to despise anyone
    wise but poor,
    nor proper to honor the lawless.
²⁴The prince, the ruler, the judge are
    in honor;
    but none is greater than the one
        who fears God.
²⁵When the free serve a wise slave,
    the wise will not complain.
²⁶Do not flaunt your wisdom in
    managing your affairs,
    or boast in your time of need.
²⁷Better the worker who has goods
    in plenty
    than the boaster who has no food.

²⁸My son, with humility have self-
    esteem;
    and give yourself the esteem you
        deserve.
²⁹Who will acquit those who con-
    demn themselves?
    Who will honor those who dis-
        grace themselves?

³⁰The poor are honored for their
    wisdom;
    the rich are honored for their
        wealth.

³¹Honored in poverty, how much
    more so in wealth!
    Disgraced in wealth, in poverty
        how much the more!

11 ¹The wisdom of the poor lifts
    their head high
    and sets them among princes.
²Do not praise anyone for good looks;
    or despise anyone because of
        appearance.

³The bee is least among winged
    creatures,
    but it reaps the choicest of
        harvests.
⁴Do not mock the one who wears
    only a loin-cloth,
    or scoff at a person's bitter day.
For strange are the deeds of the LORD,
    hidden from mortals his work.
⁵Many are the oppressed who rise
    to the throne;
    some that none would consider
        wear a crown.
⁶Many are the exalted who fall into
    utter disgrace,
    many the honored who are
        given into the power of
        the few.

Next, Ben Sira advises his students to have a realistic and positive appreciation of their own value (10:28-29), because no one will honor those who discredit themselves. Honor is available to the impoverished for their prudence, whereas the rich easily gain prestige through their wealth. A pauper's wisdom can lead to a position of honor among princes.

In 11:2-6 Ben Sira observes that appearances can be deceptive (1 Sam 16:7; Isa 11:3), since even a tiny bee can produce the sweetest honey. Sirach 11:4-6 is a reminder that God can bring about unexpected reversals in human situations (10:14). People can go from prison to become national leaders (Eccl 4:14). A biblical case is the patriarch Joseph (Gen 41:14-44), while a late twentieth-century example is Nelson Mandela of South Africa. By contrast, powerful dictators can be overthrown.

Moderation and Patience

⁷Before investigating, do not find
fault;
examine first, then criticize.
⁸Before listening, do not say a word,
interrupt no one in the midst of
speaking.
⁹Do not dispute about what is not
your concern;
in the quarrels of the arrogant do
not take part.

¹⁰My son, why increase your anxiety,
since whoever is greedy for wealth
will not be blameless?
Even if you chase after it, you will
never overtake it;
and by fleeing you will not
escape.
¹¹One may work and struggle and
drive,
and fall short all the same.
¹²Others go their way broken-down
drifters,
with little strength and great
misery—
Yet the eye of the LORD looks favorably upon them,

shaking them free of the stinking
mire.
¹³He lifts up their heads and exalts
them
to the amazement of the many.

¹⁴Good and evil, life and death,
poverty and riches—all are from
the LORD.
¹⁷The Lord's gift remains with the
devout;
his favor brings lasting success.
¹⁸Some become rich through a
miser's life,
and this is their allotted reward:
¹⁹When they say: "I have found rest,
now I will feast on my goods,"
They do not know how long it will
be
till they die and leave them to
others.

²⁰My child, stand by your agreement
and attend to it,
grow old while doing your work.
²¹Do not marvel at the works of a
sinner,
but trust in the LORD and wait
for his light;

11:7-28 Moderation

Wishing to encourage thoughtfulness in his students, Ben Sira urges them to beware of criticizing others on the basis of preconceived judgments. Instead, they are to get the facts first and listen without interrupting (Prov 18:13). In 11:9 the sage urges them to stick humbly to their own business (3:21-23), without getting caught up in conflicts among the powerful (Prov 26:17). Sirach 11:10 asserts that those desperate to get rich cannot help sinning (Prov 28:20; 1 Tim 6:10), because their thirst for wealth is insatiable (Eccl 5:9).

Ben Sira then makes a contrast (11:11-13): one person may toil hard yet not attain success (Eccl 9:11), while a weak person may rise in the world because of God's blessing. Sirach 11:14 draws the conclusion: both success and failure are in God's hands. Thomas à Kempis (1380–1471) develops this biblical teaching (Prov 16:9; 19:21): "Humanity proposes, but God

For it is easy in the eyes of the LORD
 suddenly, in an instant, to make
 the poor rich.

²²God's blessing is the lot of the
 righteous,
 and in due time their hope bears
 fruit.
²³Do not say: "What do I need?
 What further benefits can be
 mine?"
²⁴Do not say: "I am self-sufficient.
 What harm can come to me
 now?"
²⁵The day of prosperity makes one
 forget adversity;
 the day of adversity makes one
 forget prosperity.

²⁶For it is easy for the Lord on the
 day of death
 to repay mortals according to
 their conduct.

²⁷A time of affliction brings forget-
 fulness of past delights;
 at the end of life one's deeds are
 revealed.
²⁸Call none happy before death,
 for how they end, they are
 known.

Care in Choosing Friends

²⁹Not everyone should be brought
 into your house,
 for many are the snares of the
 crafty.
³⁰Like a decoy partridge in a cage,
 so is the heart of the proud,
 and like a spy they will pick out
 the weak spots.
³¹For they lie in wait to turn good
 into evil,
 and to praiseworthy deeds they
 attach blame.
³²One spark kindles many coals;
 a sinner lies in wait for blood.

disposes" (*Imitation of Christ* 1.19). In view of the inevitability of death, it is stupid to be miserly (14:3-12). Comparable teaching appears in Ecclesiastes 5:12–6:2, and in Jesus' parable of the rich fool (Luke 12:16-21).

In 11:20 Ben Sira advocates concentrating on one's own task instead of being fascinated by the apparent success of sinners (9:11). In due course God can reward anyone who patiently trusts in God (Ps 37:1-3).

Sirach 11:23-24 refutes the claims of those seeking to live self-sufficiently, independent of God. As good times can make one forget the lessons of adversity, so hard times can blot out the happiness of earlier prosperity. The Hebrew text of Sirach has no place for retribution in the afterlife. Instead, the sage warns that God can repay the evildoer with a miserable death (11:26-27). Hence 11:28 echoes the saying of the sixth-century B.C. Greek poet Solon: "Until he is dead, do not yet call a person happy, but only lucky" (Herodotus, *Histories* 1.32).

11:29–12:18 Warnings about strangers, beggars, and enemies

Sirach 11:29-34, doubtless based on observation and bitter experience, warns against strangers taking advantage of hospitality. Talebearers will turn good to evil, and their words will start a whole fire leading to disas-

³³Beware of scoundrels, for they
    breed only evil,
and they may give you a lasting
    stain.
³⁴Admit strangers into your home,
    and they will stir up trouble
and make you a stranger to your
    own family.
12 ¹If you do good, know for whom
    you are doing it,
and your kindness will have its
    effect.
²Do good to the righteous and
    reward will be yours,
if not from them, from the LORD.
³No good comes to those who give
    comfort to the wicked,
nor is it an act of mercy that
    they do.
⁴Give to the good but refuse the
    sinner;
⁵refresh the downtrodden but give
    nothing to the proud.
No arms for combat should you
    give them,
lest they use these against you;

Twofold evil you will obtain for
    every good deed you do for
    them.
⁶For God also hates sinners,
    and takes vengeance on evil-
    doers.

⁸In prosperity we cannot know our
    friends;
in adversity an enemy will not
    remain concealed.
⁹When one is successful even an
    enemy is friendly;
but in adversity even a friend
    disappears.
¹⁰Never trust your enemies,
    for their wickedness is like cor-
    rosion in bronze.
¹¹Even though they act deferentially
    and peaceably toward you,
take care to be on your guard
    against them.
Treat them as those who reveal
    secrets,
and be certain that in the end
    there will still be envy.

---

trous results (Jas 3:5-6). A wicked person will bring forth only evil (Luke 6:45), and a stranger can alienate people from their community.

In 12:1-6 Ben Sira advises a narrow realism in almsgiving. Whereas the good will benefit from generosity, kindness to bad persons will have only harmful effects. In a comparable way, a Greek poet asserts: "Doing a good turn to the inferior is an utterly useless act of kindness" (Theognis 105). While God will reward almsgiving to a good person, Ben Sira sees no merit in giving to an evildoer.

The sage justifies his teaching by asserting God's hatred of wicked persons (12:6). The Qumran community also saw as its task "to detest all the children of darkness, each one in accordance with his blame in God's vindication" (1QS 1.10-11). However, Wisdom 11:24 asserts God's love for all creation. As a whole, Sirach 12:1-6 offers a contrast with the Sermon on the Mount, where Jesus affirms God's loving care of the wicked as well as the good, and the consequent duty of his disciples to love evildoers as well as good persons (Matt 5:44-45).

¹²Do not let them stand near you,
 lest they push you aside and
  take your place.
Do not let them sit at your right
  hand,
 or they will demand your seat,
And in the end you will appreciate
  my advice,
 when you groan with regret,
  as I warned.

¹³Who pities a snake charmer when
  he is bitten,
 or anyone who goes near a wild
  beast?
¹⁴So it is with the companion of the
  proud,
 who is involved in their sins:
¹⁵While you stand firm, they make
  no move;
 but if you slip, they cannot hold
  back.
¹⁶With their lips enemies speak
  sweetly,

but in their heart they scheme to
  plunge you into the abyss.
Though enemies have tears in their
  eyes,
 given the chance, they will never
  have enough of your blood.
¹⁷If evil comes upon you, you will
  find them at hand;
 pretending to help, they will
  trip you up,
¹⁸Then they will shake their heads
  and clap their hands
 and hiss repeatedly, and show
  their true faces.

Caution Regarding Associates

13 ¹Touch pitch and you blacken
  your hand;
 associate with scoundrels and
  you learn their ways.
²Do not lift a weight too heavy for
  you,
 or associate with anyone
  wealthier than you.

Ben Sira observes that we recognize our true friends only in adversity (12:8-9), when fair-weather friends disappear (Prov 19:4). A Greek poet makes a similar observation: "No one wants to be a friend whenever hard times befall a person" (Theognis 299). In 12:10-12 Ben Sira warns his students to be cautious, or else someone hostile may usurp their place.

Sirach 12:13-14 plays on the Hebrew word *hober*, which can mean "snake charmer" or "companion." Just as no one pities a snake charmer who is bitten (Eccl 10:11), so an associate of someone proud will also suffer painful treatment. In 12:16 Ben Sira contrasts an enemy's pleasant words with the scheming in his heart (Prov 6:12-14; 26:24). In adversity the false friend will cause one's downfall, even while pretending to help. Sirach 12:18 mentions the traditional gestures of mockery with which the enemy will make fun of one's humiliation (Ps 22:8; Lam 2:15).

13:1-23 Caution toward the rich and powerful

The next poem urges caution in choosing associates. The opening proverb takes a lesson from the natural world: just as people cannot touch pitch without getting their hands covered in the sticky substance, so a scoffer's

How can the clay pot go with the
metal cauldron?
When they knock together, the
pot will be smashed:
³The rich do wrong and boast of it,
while the poor are wronged and
beg forgiveness.
⁴As long as the rich can use you
they will enslave you,
but when you are down and out
they will abandon you.
⁵As long as you have anything they
will live with you,
but they will drain you dry
without remorse.
⁶When they need you they will
deceive you
and smile at you and raise your
hopes;
they will speak kindly to you and
say, "What do you need?"
⁷They will embarrass you at their
dinner parties,
and finally laugh at you.

Afterwards, when they see you,
they will pass you by,
and shake their heads at you.
⁸Be on guard: do not act too boldly;
do not be like those who lack
sense.

⁹When the influential draw near,
keep your distance;
then they will urge you all the
more.
¹⁰Do not draw too close, lest you be
rebuffed,
but do not keep too far away
lest you be regarded as
an enemy.
¹¹Do not venture to be free with
them,
do not trust their many words;
For by prolonged talk they will test
you,
and though smiling they will
probe you.
¹²Mercilessly they will make you a
laughingstock,

---

companion will learn his way of behaving. Likewise, a Greek poet warns
against mixing with persons regarded as inferior: "If you mingle with the
base, you will lose even the sense you have" (Theognis 35-36).

Associating with a richer person is like trying to carry something too
heavy (13:2). Whereas the rich can get away with their crimes, the poor
always have to ask for forgiveness (Prov 18:23). The wealthy can exploit the
poor and then abandon them. Therefore, 13:8 warns against the senseless
presumption of mixing with richer people (Prov 25:6-7; Luke 14:8-11).

A moderate humility is the best response to an invitation from the influential (13:9-13). Someone inordinately keen to approach them can risk
outright rejection, while someone excessively reticent risks being left behind
altogether. After using words to test one (13:11), the influential person will
readily inflict mockery or punishment. Hence the sage advises his students
to avoid keeping company with the powerful ruling class.

In the next part (13:15-20) Ben Sira utilizes comparisons from the animal
world to inculcate caution. Like the Greek fables of Aesop, the Hebrew
Bible sometimes employs animal imagery for people (Ezek 22:25-27; Ps

and will not refrain from injury
or chains.
¹³Be on your guard and take care
never to accompany lawless
people.

¹⁵Every living thing loves its own
kind,
and we all love someone like
ourselves.
¹⁶Every living being keeps close to
its own kind;
and people associate with their
own kind.
¹⁷Is a wolf ever allied with a lamb?
So the sinner with the righteous.
¹⁸Can there be peace between the
hyena and the dog?
Or peace between the rich and
the poor?
¹⁹Wild donkeys of the desert are
lion's prey;
likewise the poor are feeding
grounds for the rich.

²⁰Humility is an abomination to the
proud;
and the poor are an abomination
to the rich.
²¹When the rich stumble they are
supported by friends;
when the poor trip they are
pushed down by friends.
²²When the rich speak they have
many supporters;
though what they say is repugnant, it wins approval.
When the poor speak people say,
"Come, come, speak up!"
though they are talking sense,
they get no hearing.
²³When the rich speak all are silent,
their wisdom people extol to the
clouds.
When the poor speak people say:
"Who is that?"
If they stumble, people knock
them down.

22:21-22). According to 13:15-16, it is natural for a human being to like someone similar. Aristotle (d. 322 B.C.) also observes: "We love those who are like ourselves" (*Nicomachean Ethics* 8.1.6). Hence Ben Sira recommends associating with one's own kind.

Sirach 13:17-19 contrasts the innocent parties (lamb, dog, wild donkey) with the predators (wolf, hyena, lion). Ben Sira first uses the proverbial comparison between wolf and lamb (Isa 11:6; Matt 10:16) to show the impossibility of allying sinners with innocent persons (2 Cor 6:14-15). Although Near Eastern street dogs could be wild, they were not as fierce as hyenas seeking food. Hence Ben Sira makes this second comparison to contrast the poor and the rich in their struggle to survive, marked by an economic "survival of the fittest." In 13:19 Ben Sira draws a third contrast between the wild donkeys of the desert and the predatory lion (Job 24:4-5). The parallelism suggests that he links the rich with evildoing and sees the poor as tending to be innocent victims (34:21-24).

Sirach 13:21-23 extends the contrast between rich and poor by describing general reactions to them. People rush to help a rich person who stumbles,

²⁴Wealth is good where there is no sin;
  but poverty is evil by the standards of the proud.
²⁵The heart changes one's face,
  either for good or for evil.
²⁶The sign of a good heart is a radiant face;
  withdrawn and perplexed is the toiling schemer.

14 ¹Happy those whose mouth causes them no grief,
  those who are not stung by remorse for sin.
²Happy are those whose conscience does not reproach them,
those who have not lost hope.

The Use of Wealth

³Wealth is not appropriate for the mean-spirited;
  to misers, what use is gold?
⁴What they deny themselves they collect for someone else,
  and strangers will live sumptuously on their possessions.
⁵To whom will they be generous that are stingy with themselves
  and do not enjoy what is their own?
⁶None are worse than those who are stingy with themselves;
  they punish their own avarice.
⁷If ever they do good, it is by mistake;

---

but in a similar situation they push down someone poor (Prov 14:20; 19:4). Likewise, people acclaim the unsavory words of the wealthy, but shove aside the poor even if they speak sensibly (Eccl 9:15-16).

13:24–14:19 The use of wealth

Ben Sira's discussion of the proper use of material goods begins with the statement that wealth can be good for the sinless person (31:8-11). Sirach 13:25-26 suggests that people's generosity (or otherwise) can be seen on their faces (Prov 15:13; Eccl 8:1). According to 14:1-2, depression from having said or done harmful things can spoil a person's happiness (22:22; 28:26).

In 14:3-10 Ben Sira describes the sad situation of misers, who actually gain no benefit from their wealth (Prov 28:22). Indeed, the money they save will be spent by other people (Eccl 6:2-3)! Sirach 14:5 observes that those unable to be kind to themselves find it hard to be generous to others (10:28-29; 11:18-19). By their miserliness they punish only themselves (Eccl 5:9-12). Misers cannot even enjoy the food that they eagerly acquire, since they are not contented with what they have (Prov 30:8-9; 1 Tim 6:8).

Since death is inevitable (14:11-12), it is good to enjoy life while it lasts (Eccl 8:15). Using God's good gifts is not mere self-indulgence if it involves sharing with friends. Instead of leaving wealth to others, Ben Sira urges present enjoyment of it (Eccl 2:18-24). His lack of expectation of an afterlife (matching Eccl 9:9-10) contrasts with the hope of immortality expressed in the book of Wisdom (Wis 3:1-9).

in the end they reveal their meanness.
⁸Misers are evil people,
they turn away and disregard others.
⁹The greedy see their share as not enough;
greedy injustice dries up the soul.
¹⁰The eye of the miserly is rapacious for food,
but there is none of it on their own table.

¹¹My son, if you have the means, treat yourself well,
and enjoy life as best you can.
¹²Remember that death does not delay,
and you have not been told the grave's appointed time.
¹³Before you die, be good to your friends;
give them a share in what you possess.
¹⁴Do not deprive yourself of good things now
or let a choice portion escape you.

¹⁵Will you not leave your riches to others,
and your earnings to be divided by lot?
¹⁶Give and take, treat yourself well,
for in Sheol there are no joys to seek.
¹⁷All flesh grows old like a garment;
the age-old law is: everyone must die.
¹⁸As with the leaves growing on a luxuriant tree—
one falls off and another sprouts—
So with the generations of flesh and blood:
one dies and another flourishes.
¹⁹All human deeds surely perish;
the works they do follow after them.

The Search for Wisdom and Her Blessings

²⁰Happy those who meditate on Wisdom,
and fix their gaze on knowledge;

Sirach 14:17-19 (like 41:3-4) speaks further about nature's law of death (Gen 2:17; 3:19). The image of the garment wearing out is biblical (Isa 51:6; Ps 102:27). The comparison of human generations with leaves on a tree (Job 14:7-10) occurs also in Homer's *Iliad* (6.146-149).

WISDOM IN SPEECH AND THOUGHT

Sirach 14:20–23:27

14:20–15:10 The blessings of searching for wisdom

The opening beatitude speaks of the happiness of one who meditates on wisdom (Ps 1:1-2). A Qumran poem makes a similar statement: "Happy is the person who attains Wisdom, and walks in the law of the Most High, and dedicates his heart to her ways" (4Q525 2.2.3-4). In 14:21-27 wisdom is personified as a woman. The sage urges his students to seek wisdom as

²¹Who ponder her ways in their heart,
and understand her paths;
²²Who pursue her like a scout,
and watch at her entry way;
²³Who peep through her windows,
and listen at her doors;
²⁴Who encamp near her house
and fasten their tent pegs next to her walls;
²⁵Who pitch their tent beside her,
and dwell in a good place;
²⁶Who build their nest in her leaves,
and lodge in her branches;
²⁷Who take refuge from the heat in her shade
and dwell in her home.

15 ¹Whoever fears the LORD will do this;
whoever is practiced in the Law will come to Wisdom.
²She will meet him like a mother;
like a young bride she will receive him,
³She will feed him with the bread of learning,
and give him the water of understanding to drink.
⁴He will lean upon her and not fall;
he will trust in her and not be put to shame.
⁵She will exalt him above his neighbors,
and in the assembly she will make him eloquent.
⁶Joy and gladness he will find,
and an everlasting name he will inherit.
⁷The worthless will not attain her,
and the haughty will not behold her.
⁸She is far from the impious;
liars never think of her.
⁹Praise is unseemly on the lips of sinners,
for it has not been allotted to them by God.
¹⁰But praise is uttered by the mouth of the wise,
and its rightful owner teaches it.

---

assiduously as a young man courting his girlfriend, waiting patiently beside her house (Prov 8:34) and even looking through the window to see her (Song 2:9). Indeed, there is a progression from observing where wisdom dwells (14:22-23) to encamping near her house (14:24-25), and then setting up home with her as his bride (14:26; 15:2). In 14:26-27 wisdom is portrayed as a tree (Prov 3:18), providing refuge from the burning heat (Isa 4:6).

According to 15:1, wisdom is available to the God-fearing person who keeps the Torah (1:26; 19:20). Ben Sira declares that wisdom will be as caring as a mother (Isa 49:15; 66:13) and as loving as a young bride for the male student (Prov 5:18). Sirach 15:3 states that she will feed him with understanding (Isa 30:20; Prov 9:1-6). In old age he will be able to lean on her when he finds walking difficult. Wisdom will also grant eloquence to those who love her (Wis 8:10-11). This wisdom is as much moral as intellectual, not available to the impious or the arrogant (15:7-8) who reject God's words

Free Will

◀ ¹¹Do not say: "It was God's doing
     that I fell away,"
 for what he hates he does not do.
¹²Do not say: "He himself has led me
     astray,"
 for he has no need of the wicked.
¹³Abominable wickedness the LORD
     hates
 and he does not let it happen to
     those who fear him.

¹⁴God in the beginning created
     human beings
 and made them subject to their
     own free choice.
¹⁵If you choose, you can keep the
     commandments;

 loyalty is doing the will of God.
¹⁶Set before you are fire and water;
 to whatever you choose, stretch
     out your hand.
¹⁷Before everyone are life and death,
 whichever they choose will be
     given them.

¹⁸Immense is the wisdom of the LORD;
 mighty in power, he sees all
     things.
¹⁹The eyes of God behold his works,
 and he understands every
     human deed.
²⁰He never commands anyone to
     sin,
 nor shows leniency toward
     deceivers.

(Ps 50:16-17). The wise person is characterized by a readiness to praise God (Ps 33:1).

15:11-20 Human free will

A perennial theological puzzle lies in the balance between human free will and divine predestination. Whereas Genesis 3 narrates the sin of Adam and Eve after the serpent's temptation, some Jewish apocalyptic circles traced back the origin of sin to the fallen angels (1 Enoch 6:1–9:9), while various Greek writers blamed human shortcomings on fate. In 15:11-20 Ben Sira wishes to emphasize human responsibility in contrast to those who denied liability for their actions. Sirach 15:11 teaches that human sin cannot derive from God (Jas 1:13), who does not cause human beings to do things that God dislikes (Wis 11:24).

After creating human beings (15:14), God gave them into the power of their free choice, an inclination either to good or to evil (Gen 2:16-17). Human beings are capable of fulfilling the divine commands (Deut 30:11-14), because God does not demand what is impossible. Sirach 15:16-17 spells out the choice offered to human beings: either life or death (Deut 30:15; Jer 21:8), symbolized by life-giving water or destructive fire (3:30). God's commands are not narrow or stifling, because divine wisdom is immense, but God's eyes see every human deed (Prov 15:3; Heb 4:13). In conclusion, God never commands sin or authorizes deceit.

God's Punishment of Sinners

16 ¹Do not yearn for worthless children,
or rejoice in wicked offspring.
²Even if they be many, do not rejoice in them
if they do not have fear of the LORD.
³Do not count on long life for them,
or have any hope for their future.
For one can be better than a thousand;
rather die childless than have impious children!
⁴Through one wise person a city can be peopled;
but through a clan of rebels it becomes desolate.

⁵Many such things my eye has seen,
and even more than these my ear has heard.
⁶Against a sinful band fire is kindled,
upon a godless people wrath blazes.
⁷He did not forgive the princes of old who rebelled long ago in their might.
⁸He did not spare the neighbors of Lot,
abominable in their pride.
⁹He did not spare the doomed people,
dispossessed because of their sin;
¹⁰Nor the six hundred thousand foot soldiers,
sent to their graves for the arrogance of their hearts.

16:1-23 God's punishment of sinners

Sirach 16:1-4 considers what kinds of children are desirable. Ancient Israelite society viewed children as a sign of divine blessing (Deut 28:4; Ps 128:1-4) and childlessness as a curse (Deut 28:18; 1 Sam 1:6). Sinners with many children could therefore claim that they had God's blessing. What impresses Ben Sira, however, is not the quantity of children but the quality of their lives. Having numerous children is no cause for joy unless they are God-fearing (Wis 3:10-12; 4:3-6). Better a virtuous person who is childless than the parent of godless children (Prov 17:21; Wis 4:1).

Sirach 16:5-10 discusses examples of divine punishment (2 Pet 2:4-9; 3 Macc 2:4-7), as a warning to sinners not to presume on God's forgiveness. Thus, fire burned up Korah's rebellious group (Num 16:35), the ancient giants did not receive the divine pardon (Gen 6:4; Bar 3:26-28), and God did not spare Lot's proud neighbors from punishment (Gen 19:24-25). Moreover, Joshua placed the doomed Canaanites under the ban (Deut 7:1-2; Josh 11:16-20). In 16:9 the sage assumes the sinfulness of the Holy Land's early inhabitants (Gen 15:16; 1 Kgs 21:26), though modern readers might regret the placing of nationalistic limits on God's universal mercy. Like the Canaanites, the Israelites could not presume on divine compassion. Sirach 16:10 refers to the six hundred thousand Israelite males (46:8) who died in

¹¹Had there been but one stiff-necked
person,
it would be a wonder had he
gone unpunished.
For mercy and anger alike are with
him;
he remits and forgives, but also
pours out wrath.
¹²Great as his mercy is his punishment;
he judges people, each according
to their deeds.
¹³Criminals do not escape with their
plunder;
the hope of the righteous, God
never leaves unfulfilled.
¹⁴Whoever does good has a reward;
each receives according to their
deeds.

¹⁷Do not say: "I am hidden from God;
and on high who remembers
me?

Among so many people I am un-
known;
what am I in the world of spirits?
¹⁸Look, the heavens and the highest
heavens,
the abyss and the earth tremble
at his visitation.
¹⁹The roots of the mountains and the
earth's foundations—
at his mere glance they quiver
and quake.
²⁰Of me, therefore, he will take no
notice;
with my ways who will be concerned?
²¹If I sin, no eye will see me;
if all in secret I act deceitfully,
who is to know?
²²Who tells him about just deeds?
What can I expect for doing my
duty?"
²³Such the thoughts of the senseless;
only the foolish entertain them.

the wilderness as a punishment for their unfaithfulness (Num 11:21; 14:26-30). Hence, if whole nations have been punished for rebelliousness, how much more should an individual avoid being irreligious!

According to 16:11, the wise recognize that God can be angry as well as merciful (5:6). God is capable of punishing sinners and rectifying injustice (16:12-13). The righteous person can be confident of eventually receiving a reward (51:30), even if present experience offers no sign of it. Two supplementary verses (16:15-16), found in some manuscripts, specify the unbelieving Pharaoh (Exod 7:3-4) as an example of a sinner.

Sirach 16:17-23 teaches that sinners cannot escape the eye of God, who punishes iniquity. Here Ben Sira refutes an opponent's view that human beings are too insignificant for God to take an interest in their faults (Ps 8:4-6; Jer 23:24). "If God's dominion extends through the vast universe," asks the skeptic, "will the Almighty bother to pay attention to my ways?" This opponent believes that God notices neither sins nor good deeds (Ps 10:11; Isa 29:15), but Ben Sira knows that God sees everything (23:18-19).

Divine Wisdom Seen in Creation

²⁴Listen to me, my son, and take my
advice,
and apply your mind to my
words,
²⁵While I pour out my spirit by
measure
and impart knowledge with care.
²⁶When at the first God created his
works
and, as he made them, assigned
their tasks,
²⁷He arranged for all time what they
were to do,
their domains from generation to
generation.
They were not to go hungry or
grow weary,
or ever cease from their tasks.
²⁸Never does a single one crowd its
neighbor,
or do any ever disobey his word.
²⁹Then the Lord looked upon the
earth,
and filled it with his blessings.
³⁰Its surface he covered with every
kind of living creature
which must return into it again.

16:24–17:24 Divine wisdom seen in creation

According to 16:26-30, divine providence is evident from the creation (Ps 104:24; Rom 1:20). God's ordering of the universe provides for the needs of each created thing (39:33-34), and the world is governed by the divine word (Ps 147:18; 148:8). The sage's emphasis on the purposefulness of creation reflects biblical tradition (Ps 148:6; Jer 31:35-36), and also agrees with Stoic philosophy. While animals cover the earth in fulfillment of God's blessing (Gen 1:22), nevertheless they are mortal (14:17-18) and will return to the earth (Ps 104:29).

Sirach 17:1-14 deals with God's making of human beings. Their creation from the earth echoes Genesis 2:7, while their return to it in death recalls Genesis 3:19. While Genesis 3 sees death as a divine punishment for human sin, Ben Sira regards death as God's decree (41:3-4) and the providential completion of an allotted number of days (37:25; 41:13). God's gift to humanity of authority over creation recalls Genesis 1:28 and Psalm 8:6, while the making of them in God's image draws on Genesis 1:27. Animals' fear of humans is reminiscent of Genesis 9:2.

Sirach 17:6 varies the Greek notion of the five senses (Aristotle, *On the Soul* 2.5-12). While seeing and hearing are shared with animals, human beings have tongues not only for tasting but also for speaking. This power of speech, a capacity unique to humanity, appears in Genesis 2:20, where Adam names the animals. Instead of smell and touch, Ben Sira mentions discernment and a mind for thinking. The ability to distinguish between good and evil is an attribute of wisdom (Isa 7:15; 1 Kgs 3:9), which Adam and Eve lacked, despite the serpent's claim (Gen 3:5). Yet God enables

Creation of Human Beings

17 [1]The Lord created human beings from the earth,
and makes them return to earth again.
[2]A limited number of days he gave them,
but granted them authority over everything on earth.
[3]He endowed them with strength like his own,
and made them in his image.
[4]He put fear of them in all flesh,
and gave them dominion over beasts and birds.
[6]Discernment, tongues, and eyes, ears, and a mind for thinking he gave them.
[7]With knowledge and understanding he filled them;
good and evil he showed them.
[8]He put fear of him into their hearts to show them the grandeur of his works,
[9]That they might describe the wonders of his deeds
[10]and praise his holy name.
[11]He set before them knowledge, and allotted to them the law of life.
[12]An everlasting covenant he made with them,
and his commandments he revealed to them.
[13]His majestic glory their eyes beheld,

---

human beings to see the divine glory reflected in the created world, and thus to praise the Creator (39:33-35; 42:15-17).

In 17:11-14 we move from the creation to the giving of the law of Moses (45:5), with its promise of life in exchange for obedience (Deut 30:15; Ezek 20:11). According to Deuteronomy 5:22-26, the Israelites saw and heard the divine glory. Sirach 17:14 may refer particularly to the Ten Commandments. The command to avoid all evil may refer to the prohibitions against idolatry and sabbath work (Deut 5:6-15), while precepts about how to treat one's neighbor occur in the second part of the Decalogue (Deut 5:16-21).

Sirach 17:15-24 speaks of Israel's national life after Sinai, with a particular focus on the people's sins. At Sinai God proposed the paths for Israel to take (Deut 10:12; 30:16). Yet human ways, even when sinful, are not hidden from God (Ps 90:8; 139:3), despite the sinner's claim in 16:17-22. The ruler assigned by God to each people may be either the civil leader (Dan 2:21; Wis 6:3), or a nation's angelic guardian (Dan 10:20). However, God rules Israel directly (Deut 32:8-9), as they are God's own possession (Exod 19:5; Deut 7:6). Therefore they cannot escape divine scrutiny, because God knows their sins (23:19) and will punish transgressors (16:11).

The care for Israel as the apple of God's eye (Deut 32:10) is the basis of Ben Sira's response to the skeptic's earlier question in 16:22. Sirach 17:22 uses language that recalls the divine concern for the leader of the postexilic

his glorious voice their ears
heard.

¹⁴He said to them, "Avoid all evil";
to each of them he gave precepts
about their neighbor.

¹⁵Their ways are ever known to him,
they cannot be hidden from his
eyes.

¹⁷Over every nation he appointed a
ruler,
but Israel is the Lord's own portion.

¹⁹All their works are clear as the sun
to him,
and his eyes are ever upon their
ways.

²⁰Their iniquities cannot be hidden
from him;
all their sins are before the Lord.

²²Human goodness is like a signet
ring with God,
and virtue he keeps like the
apple of his eye.

²³Later he will rise up and repay
them,
requiting each one as they deserve.

Appeal for a Return to God

²⁴But to the penitent he provides a
way back
and encourages those who are
losing hope!

²⁵Turn back to the Lord and give up
your sins,
pray before him and make your
offenses few.

²⁶Turn again to the Most High and
away from iniquity,
and hate intensely what he
loathes.

²⁷Who in Sheol can glorify the Most
High
in place of the living who offer
their praise?

²⁸The dead can no more give praise
than those who have never
lived;
they who are alive and well
glorify the Lord.

²⁹How great is the mercy of the Lord,
and his forgiveness for those
who return to him!

³⁰For not everything is within
human reach,

Jerusalem community, Zerubbabel (49:11), who is compared to God's signet ring (Hag 2:23). In 17:24 the sage concludes this section with the assertion (4:26; 5:7) that the repentant are offered a way back to God (Ezek 33:11).

17:25–18:14 Call to leave sin behind

This poem appeals to human beings to repent, because God is both powerful and merciful. Sirach 17:25-26 echoes the prophetic calls to repentance (Jer 3:12-14; Joel 2:12-13). By hating wickedness, humans become like God (15:13). Sirach 17:27-28 expresses the view of Hebrew writers before the Maccabean revolt that nobody can praise God after death (Ps 88:11-13; Isa 38:18). Hence, living persons need to receive the abundant divine mercy (Ps 31:20; 86:5). By contrast, mortality sets limits to human mercy (Ps 103:13-18). If God can find fault with the angels, how much more with mortals (Job 15:15-16; 25:5-6), who are merely "dust and ashes" (10:9)!

since human beings are not
immortal.
³¹Is anything brighter than the sun?
Yet it can be eclipsed.
How worthless then the thoughts
of flesh and blood!
³²God holds accountable the hosts
of highest heaven,
while all mortals are dust and
ashes.

The Divine Power and Mercy

18 ¹He who lives forever created
the whole universe;
²the Lᴏʀᴅ alone is just.
⁴To whom has he given power to
describe his works,
and who can search out his
mighty deeds?
⁵Who can measure his majestic
power,
or fully recount his mercies?
⁶No one can lessen, increase,
or fathom the wonders of the
Lord.
⁷When mortals finish, they are only
beginning,
and when they stop they are still
bewildered.

⁸What are mortals? What are they
worth?
What is good in them, and what
is evil?
⁹The number of their days seems
great
if it reaches a hundred years.
¹⁰Like a drop of water from the sea
and a grain of sand,
so are these few years among
the days of eternity.
¹¹That is why the Lord is patient with
them
and pours out his mercy on
them.
¹²He sees and understands that their
death is wretched,
and so he forgives them all the
more.
¹³Their compassion is for their
neighbor,
but the Lord's compassion
reaches all flesh,
Reproving, admonishing, teaching,
and turning them back, as a
shepherd his flock.
¹⁴He has compassion on those who
accept his discipline,
who are eager for his precepts.

Sirach 18:1-2 notes that unlike humankind, God is just (Ps 51:6-7; 145:17). Ben Sira next echoes biblical statements (Ps 145:3; Job 9:10) that no human being can fully declare the divine greatness (42:17; 43:31). No one can add to God's majesty (Eccl 3:14), or subtract from it (42:21). Unlike God, human beings are limited (Ps 8:5; 144:3). While a person's allotted lifespan may be seventy or eighty years (Ps 90:10), one hundred years is even now exceptional, yet God is everlasting (Ps 90:2).

Sirach 18:11 presumes that God's very majesty makes God compassionate (Wis 11:21-23; Ps 36:6-7). Human mortality evokes divine mercy (Ps 103:13-14). While a person will naturally be compassionate to a neighbor (13:15), God's mercy reaches out to all humanity, like a shepherd's care for a flock (Isa 40:11; Ps 23:1).

"Is anything brighter than the sun? Yet it can be eclipsed" (Sir 17:31).

The Need for Prudence

¹⁵My child, add no reproach to your
charity,
or spoil any gift by harsh words.
¹⁶Does not the dew give relief from
the scorching heat?
So a word can be better than a
gift.
¹⁷Indeed does not a word count more
than a good gift?
But both are offered by a kind
person.
¹⁸The fool is ungracious and abusive,
and a grudging gift makes the
eyes smart.

¹⁹Before you speak, learn;
before you get sick, prepare the
cure.
²⁰Before you are judged, examine
yourself,
and at the time of scrutiny you
will have forgiveness.
²¹Before you fall ill, humble yourself;

and when you have sinned, show
repentance.
Do not delay forsaking your sins;
do not neglect to do so until you
are in distress.

²²Let nothing prevent the prompt
payment of your vows;
do not wait until death to fulfill
them.
²³Before making a vow prepare
yourself;
do not be like one who puts the
Lord to the test.
²⁴Think of wrath on the day of death,
the time of vengeance when he
will hide his face.
²⁵Think of the time of hunger in the
time of plenty,
poverty and need in the day of
wealth.
²⁶Between morning and evening
there is a change of time;
before the Lord all things are
fleeting.

18:15–19:17 Prudential warnings

After a long section of theological teaching on the origin of sin (15:11–18:14), Ben Sira begins a lengthy section of ethical instruction (18:15–23:27). The present poem falls into three parts: on wise conduct (18:15-29); on control of the passions (18:30–19:4); and on the correct use of the tongue (19:5-17).

According to 18:15-18, a generous attitude when giving is as important as the gift itself; thereby we imitate our gracious God (2 Cor 9:7; Jas 1:5). A time of giving is the wrong occasion for reproving (20:1). Sirach 18:19-21 emphasizes the value of being prepared: it is better to have the cure before falling ill. Likewise, it is sensible to acknowledge one's fault repentantly, before others pass judgment (Matt 7:1; 1 Cor 11:31) and before death comes (5:7-8; 17:25). Sirach 18:22-24 urges the prompt payment of vows before death may strike (Deut 23:21-23; Eccl 5:3-4). For Ben Sira the thought of death is a motive for right conduct (28:6-7). The wise are aware that their situation in life can alter suddenly, just as the weather can quickly change.

27The wise are discreet in all things;
    where sin is rife they keep them-
      selves from wrongdoing.
28Every wise person teaches wisdom,
    and those who know her declare
      her praise;
29Those skilled in words become
    wise themselves,
    and pour forth apt proverbs.

Self-Control

30Do not let your passions be your
    guide,
    but keep your desires in check.
31If you allow yourself to satisfy
    your passions,
    they will make you the laughing-
      stock of your enemies.
32Take no pleasure in too much
    luxury
    which brings on poverty re-
      doubled.
33Do not become a glutton and a
    drunkard
    with nothing in your purse.

19

1Whoever does this grows no
    richer;
    those who waste the little they
      have will be stripped bare.
2Wine and women make the heart
    lustful,
    and the companion of prostitutes
      becomes reckless.
3Rottenness and worms will possess
    him,
    and the reckless will be snatched
      away.
4Whoever trusts others too quickly
    has a shallow mind,
    and those who sin wrong them-
      selves.

The Proper Use of Speech

5Whoever gloats over evil will be
    destroyed,
6and whoever repeats gossip has
    no sense.
7Never repeat gossip,
    and no one will reproach you.
8Tell nothing to friend or foe;

Sirach 18:30–19:4 advises control of the passions, in the tradition of Hebrew and Egyptian wisdom literature. Those who follow their appetites will end up as the laughing stock of their enemies (Prov 21:17). Gluttonous winebibbers spend money they do not have on eating and drinking (Deut 21:20; Prov 23:20-21). Proper stewardship of one's resources will prevent poverty and its associated shame (40:28-30). Wine and loose women can make a person reckless (Prov 23:31-33; 31:3-5). An admonition against mixing with prostitutes is common in the wisdom literature of Israel (Prov 5:1-6; 23:26-28), as well as in Egypt.

In 19:5-12 the sage urges discipline in speech (5:14–6:1; 22:27–23:3). A person can escape reproach by refusing to repeat an evil report (Prov 25:9-10) and keeping a discreet silence instead. In contrast to the misuse of the tongue to reveal the faults of others inappropriately, Ben Sira advocates a proper use of speech to admonish friends and neighbors (19:13-17). The biblical command to point out the faults of others (Lev 19:17) was taken seriously by many Jewish groups around the first century. Both Jesus and

and unless it be a sin for you, do
not reveal a thing.
⁹For someone may have heard you
and watched you,
and in time come to hate you.
¹⁰Let anything you hear die with
you;
never fear, it will not make you
burst!
¹¹Having heard something, the fool
goes into labor,
like a woman giving birth to a
child.
¹²Like an arrow stuck in a fool's
thigh,
so is gossip in the belly of a fool.
¹³Admonish your friend—he may
not have done it;
and if he did, that he may not
do it again.

¹⁴Admonish your neighbor—he may
not have said it;
and if he did, that he may not say
it again.
¹⁵Admonish your friend—often it
may be slander;
do not believe every story.
¹⁶Then, too, a person can slip and
not mean it;
who has not sinned with his
tongue?
¹⁷Admonish your neighbor before
you break with him;
and give due place to the Law of
the Most High.

How to Recognize True Wisdom
²⁰All wisdom is fear of the LORD;
and in all wisdom, the observance
of the Law.

---

the Qumran community laid down procedures for reproving community members (Matt 18:15-17; 1QS 5.24–6.1). Warning a friend or neighbor may stop the person reoffending (19:13-14). Yet a report of wrongdoing may be false: the wise person will not believe everything said (Prov 14:15; Eccl 7:21). Further caution is needed because an offense may be unintentional, and no one is sinless (Eccl 7:20; Ps 143:2). Instead of allowing an unchecked hurt to cause the end of a friendship, a gentle reproof is advisable (Prov 27:5-6), in accordance with the stipulation of Leviticus 19:17. Some later manuscripts have a scribal addition about fearing God and keeping the law (19:18-19).

19:20–20:31 Wisdom and folly in word and deed

Mention of the Torah in 19:17 leads the sage to point out the necessity for the wise person to follow God's law (19:20). True wisdom needs to be directed to a good purpose, because knowing how to be wicked is not wisdom at all. It is better to be considered a fool for keeping free from sin than to cleverly misuse knowledge (19:23). Vigilance is also required, because the wicked person can stealthily gain an advantage (12:10-18). However, aspects of a person's appearance will often indicate whether someone is wise or foolish (13:25-26).

²²The knowledge of wickedness is
not wisdom,
nor is there prudence in the
counsel of sinners.
²³There is a shrewdness that is de-
testable,
while the fool may be free from
sin.
²⁴Better are the God-fearing who
have little understanding
than those of great intelligence
who violate the Law.

²⁵There is a shrewdness keen but
dishonest,
and there are those who are
duplicitous to win a judgment.

²⁶There is the villain bowed in grief,
but full of deceit within.
²⁷He hides his face and pretends not
to hear,
but when not observed, he will
take advantage of you:
²⁸Even if his lack of strength keeps
him from sinning,
when he finds the right time he
will do harm.
²⁹People are known by their appearance;
the sensible are recognized as
such when first met.
³⁰One's attire, hearty laughter, and
gait
proclaim him for what he is.

Sirach 20:1-3 discusses the benefits and limits of correcting others. Whereas 19:13-17 encourages prompt reproof of an erring friend, 20:1 notes that some circumstances call for silence rather than a rebuke. Sirach 20:5-8 deals with silence and speech, a favorite theme of ancient wisdom teachers (Eccl 3:7). Silence is appropriate if one has nothing to say (Prov 17:28), or if an answer would be inappropriate at that time (5:12).

In 20:9-12 Ben Sira contrasts appearance and reality, since things are not always what they seem. An experience of failure can lead a person to greater success in the future, while a person's life may be ruined by an apparent success (such as winning the lottery today). Whereas in the ancient orient bribes were intended to benefit the giver (Prov 17:8), some gifts produce no advantage. Because God can raise people up or cast them down (7:11; 11:5), someone may rise "from rags to riches" or from humiliation to honor; see the story of the patriarch Joseph in Genesis 37–50, or Mary's song in Luke 1:47-53.

According to 20:13, wise speech makes one accepted, as Abigail found in 1 Samuel 25:23-34, whereas a fool's words are useless. By expecting too quickly an equivalent reward for kind deeds, fools will be disappointed in friendship. Sirach 20:18 resembles a saying attributed to the Stoic philoso- pher Zeno of Citium (d. 263 B.C.): "Better to slip with the foot than with the tongue" (Diogenes Laertius 7.26). A fool's proverb is unacceptable because

Conduct of the Wise and the Foolish

20 [1]There is an admonition that is untimely,
but the silent person is the wise one.
[2]It is much better to admonish than to lose one's temper;
[3]one who admits a fault will be kept from disgrace.
[4]Like a eunuch lusting to violate a young woman
is the one who does right under compulsion.
[5]One is silent and is thought wise;
another, for being talkative, is disliked.
[6]One is silent, having nothing to say;
another is silent, biding his time.
[7]The wise remain silent till the right time comes,
but a boasting fool misses the proper time.
[8]Whoever talks too much is detested;
whoever pretends to authority is hated.

[9]There is the misfortune that brings success;
and there is the gain that turns into loss.

[10]There is the gift that profits you nothing,
and there is the gift that must be paid back double.
[11]There is the loss for the sake of glory,
and there is the one who rises above humble circumstances.
[12]There is one who buys much for little,
but pays for it seven times over.
[13]The wise make themselves beloved by a few words,
but the courtesies of fools are wasted.
[14]A gift from a fool will do you no good,
for in his eyes this one gift is equal to many.
[15]He gives little, criticizes often,
and opens his mouth like a town crier.
He lends today and asks for it tomorrow;
such a person is hateful.
[16]A fool says, "I have no friends nor thanks for my generosity."
Those who eat his bread have a mocking tongue.

---

it is uttered on the wrong occasion (Prov 26:9). According to 20:21-23, a false sense of shame can cause harm (4:21), while lying deservedly causes disgrace (Prov 12:22; 13:5).

Sirach 20:27-31 returns to the theme of wisdom that opened this section (19:20-24). Wise speech will lead to advancement (Prov 22:29), as in the biblical stories of Joseph and Daniel (Gen 41:25-36; Dan 2:27-45). Just as a farmer's cultivation of land yields a harvest, so wise people's "cultivation" of their master will lead to atonement for any offenses against him (Prov 14:35). Ben Sira opposes the custom of bribery (Exod 23:8; Prov 18:16) that was widespread in the ancient orient (2 Macc 4:7-8). Concealed wisdom is as unhelpful as buried treasure (Matt 5:15-16; 25:24-30). Whereas folly is best hidden by silence (20:6), wisdom is to be revealed in speech (39:6).

¹⁷How many will ridicule him, and
how often!
¹⁸A slip on the floor is better than a
slip of the tongue;
in like manner the downfall of
the wicked comes quickly.
¹⁹A coarse person, an untimely story;
the ignorant are always ready to
offer it.
²⁰A proverb spoken by a fool is unwelcome,
for he does not tell it at the
proper time.

²¹There is a person whose poverty
prevents him from sinning,
but when he takes his rest he
has no regrets.
²²There is a person who is destroyed
through shame,
and ruined by foolish posturing.
²³There is one who promises a friend
out of shame,
and so makes an enemy needlessly.

²⁴A lie is a foul blot in a person,
yet it is always on the lips of the
ignorant.
²⁵A thief is better than an inveterate
liar,

yet both will suffer ruin.
²⁶A liar's way leads to dishonor,
and his shame remains ever
with him.

²⁷The wise gain promotion with few
words,
the prudent please the great.
²⁸Those who work the land have
abundant crops,
and those who please the great
are pardoned their faults.
²⁹Favors and gifts blind the eyes;
like a muzzle over the mouth
they silence reproofs.
³⁰Hidden wisdom and unseen
treasure—
what value has either?
³¹Better are those who hide their
folly
than those who hide their wisdom.

Dangers from Sin

21 ¹My child, if you have sinned,
do so no more,
and for your past sins pray to be
forgiven.
²Flee from sin as from a serpent
that will bite you if you go near
it;

21:1-10 Avoiding sin

Sirach 21:1-2 makes an appeal to flee from sin (17:25-26), so as not to be poisoned by its venomous bite. The mention of the serpent echoes Genesis 3:1-7, where the serpent tempts Adam and Eve. Sin has teeth as sharp as a lion's teeth; note that 1 Peter 5:8 compares the devil to a roaring lion. In another graphic image, sin is like a double-edged sword (Prov 5:4), but its antidote is God's word (Heb 4:12). In 21:4-5 Ben Sira warns against arrogant mistreatment of the poor. The proud use of terror tactics will rebound on the household of the arrogant (10:7-8), whereas God will quickly hear the prayer of the impoverished victim (35:21-25). The God-fearing person heeds warnings to repent (Prov 12:1), but boastful speakers do not recognize their faults.

Its teeth, lion's teeth,
>destroying human lives.
³All lawlessness is like a two-edged sword;
>when it cuts, there is no healing.
⁴Panic and pride wipe out wealth;
>so too the house of the proud is uprooted.
⁵Prayer from the lips of the poor is heard at once,
>and justice is quickly granted them.
⁶Whoever hates correction walks the sinner's path,
>but whoever fears the Lord repents in his heart.
⁷Glib speakers are widely known,
>but when they slip the sensible perceive it.
⁸Those who build their houses with someone else's money
>are like those who collect stones for their funeral mounds.
⁹A band of criminals is like a bundle of tow;
>they will end in a flaming fire.
¹⁰The path of sinners is smooth stones,
>but its end is the pit of Sheol.

The Wise and Foolish: A Contrast

¹¹Those who keep the Law control their thoughts;
>perfect fear of the Lord is wisdom.
¹²One who is not clever can never be taught,
>but there is a cleverness filled with bitterness.

¹³The knowledge of the wise wells up like a flood,
>and their counsel like a living spring.
¹⁴A fool's mind is like a broken jar:
>it cannot hold any knowledge at all.

¹⁵When the intelligent hear a wise saying,
>they praise it and add to it.
The wanton hear it with distaste
>and cast it behind their back.

¹⁶A fool's chatter is like a load on a journey,
>but delight is to be found on the lips of the intelligent.
¹⁷The views of the prudent are sought in an assembly,
>and their words are taken to heart.

Sirach 21:8-10 warns of the terrible consequences of sin. One who misappropriates funds to build his own house is constructing his own funerary monument (Jer 22:13-19). A criminal band is as unstable as flammable material, ready to ignite (16:6). The sinner's easy road leads to the nether world (Prov 5:5; 9:18); Ben Sira is referring to an early death rather than to eternal punishment.

21:11–22:18 Wisdom and folly

The section begins by equating observance of the Torah, fearing the Lord, and being wise. The additional element here is self-control, an important virtue in Ben Sira (22:27–23:6) as well as in St. Paul (Gal 5:23) and in Greek ethics. While one kind of cleverness helps a student to learn, another kind

"A fool's mind is like a broken jar: it cannot hold any knowledge at all" (Sir 21:14).

¹⁸Like a house in ruins is wisdom to
a fool;
to the stupid, knowledge is
incomprehensible chatter.
¹⁹To the senseless, education is fetters
on the feet,
like manacles on the right hand.
²⁰Fools raise their voice in laughter,
but the prudent at most smile
quietly.
²¹Like a gold ornament is education
to the wise,
like a bracelet on the right arm.

²²A fool steps boldly into a house,
while the well-bred are slow to
make an entrance.
²³A boor peeps through the doorway
of a house,
but the educated stay outside.
²⁴It is rude for one to listen at a door;
the discreet person would be
overwhelmed by the dis-
grace.

²⁵The lips of the arrogant talk of
what is not their concern,
but the discreet carefully weigh
their words.
²⁶The mind of fools is in their mouths,
but the mouth of the wise is in
their mind.
²⁷When the godless curse their
adversary,

they really curse themselves.
²⁸Slanderers sully themselves,
and are hated by their neighbors. ▶

On Laziness and Foolishness

22 ¹The sluggard is like a filthy
stone;
everyone hisses at his disgrace.
²The sluggard is like a lump of dung;
whoever touches it shakes it off
the hands.

³An undisciplined child is a disgrace
to its father;
if it be a daughter, she brings
him to poverty.
⁴A thoughtful daughter obtains a
husband of her own;
a shameless one is her father's
grief.
⁵A hussy shames her father and her
husband;
she is despised by both.

⁶Like music at the time of mourning
is ill-timed talk,
but lashes and discipline are at
all times wisdom.
⁷Teaching a fool is like gluing a
broken pot,
or rousing another from deep
sleep.
¹⁰Whoever talks with a fool talks to
someone asleep;

---

has only bitter fruits (19:23-25). A sage's wise teaching wells up as abun-
dantly as a spring of fresh water (24:25-31), whereas the fool's mind is like
a broken vessel (Jer 22:28), unable to contain any useful knowledge. While
the intelligent person will learn from a wise saying (Prov 9:9), the pleasure-
seeking fool simply discards it unexamined (21:15). Whereas the crafts-
person attends to skillful manual work (38:31-34), the sage pays attention
to wise public speech (39:6-8). The educational discipline that feels like a
fetter to the fool (6:29-30) is like a gold bracelet for the sensible person
(21:19-21).

when it is over, he says,
"What was that?"
¹¹Weep over the dead, for their light
has gone out;
weep over the fool, for sense has
left him.
Weep but less bitterly over the
dead, for they are at rest;
worse than death is the life of a
fool.
¹²Mourning for the dead, seven
days—
but for the wicked fool, a whole
lifetime.

¹³Do not talk much with the stupid,
or visit the unintelligent.
Beware of them lest you have
trouble
and be spattered when they
shake themselves off.

Avoid them and you will find rest
and not be wearied by their lack
of sense.
¹⁴What is heavier than lead?
What is its name but "Fool"?
¹⁵Sand, salt, and an iron weight
are easier to bear than the stupid
person.

¹⁶A wooden beam firmly bonded
into a building
is not loosened by an earthquake;
So the mind firmly resolved after
careful deliberation
will not be afraid at any time.
¹⁷The mind solidly backed by intelligent thought
is like a stucco decoration on a
smooth wall.
¹⁸Small stones lying on an open
height

Sirach 21:22-24 considers how to approach someone's home (Prov 25:17). The wise have a proper sense of reserve about entering, whereas fools brazenly enter uninvited. According to 21:26, fools speak before they think, but wise people think before speaking (Prov 14:33). Sirach 21:27-28 indicates that foul speech recoils onto the speaker. When the pagans curse the Jews (regarded as their enemies), their curse comes back on themselves (Gen 12:3; Esth 7:9-10). In attempting to besmirch the reputation of others, slanderers lose their own good name.

According to 22:1, laziness also leads to shame (Prov 24:30-34). In a vivid but disgusting image, Ben Sira then compares the sluggard to a lump of excrement that soils the hand of anyone who comes into contact with it (13:1). Sirach 22:3-6 issues warnings about unruly children. A father's natural pride in begetting a son turns to shame (16:1-2) if the son is undisciplined (Prov 17:21). Whereas Ben Sira chauvinistically considers a daughter's birth to be a loss for her parents, other biblical authors recognize that great blessings come when a woman responds to God's call (Jdt 15:9-10; Luke 1:48-49). While a sensible daughter achieves the blessing of being united with a husband (7:25), a shameless woman causes her parents grief by becoming unmarriageable (42:9-10), according to a patriarchal view of family relationships.

will not remain when the wind
blows;
So a timid mind based on foolish
plans
cannot stand up to fear of any
kind.

The Preservation of Friendship

¹⁹Whoever jabs the eye brings tears;
whoever pierces the heart bares
its feelings.
²⁰Whoever throws a stone at birds
drives them away;
whoever insults a friend breaks
up the friendship.
²¹Should you draw a sword against
a friend,
do not despair, for it can be
undone.
²²Should you open your mouth
against a friend,
do not worry, for you can be
reconciled.
But a contemptuous insult, a confidence broken,
or a treacherous attack will
drive any friend away.

²³Win your neighbor's trust while
he is poor,
so that you may rejoice with
him in his prosperity.
In time of trouble remain true to him,
so that you may share in his inheritance when it comes.

Sirach 22:9-18 employs various comparisons to describe the fool. Teaching someone unwilling to learn is no more successful than gluing together pieces of broken pottery (21:14) or trying to talk to someone who is asleep (Prov 24:33-34). As we weep for someone deceased who has gone from the sun's light (38:16), so we should mourn for the stupid person who has abandoned the light of understanding. Indeed, Ben Sira considers a fool's life to be worse than death. Whereas the customary period of mourning for the dead was traditionally a week in ancient Israel (Gen 50:10; Jdt 16:24), fools deserved to be mourned throughout their lifetime, which was a living death.

Sirach 22:13 advises against becoming the companion of someone unintelligent (the Syriac text says "pig"), so as to avoid being spattered when he shakes himself. Second Peter 2:22 also makes a comparison with a pig, which the Torah regards as an unclean animal (Lev 11:7). Sirach 22:16-18 uses building imagery to describe the solid resolve of the wise, whose firm decision will withstand an earthquake of difficulties (Ps 112:7; Matt 7:24-27), whereas the fool's timid resolve is blown away by fear of trouble.

22:19-26 Preserving friendship

Sirach 22:19-20 warns how easily insensitive behavior can destroy a friendship. In 27:9 birds serve as an image for friends gathering together, but in 22:20 and 27:19 they illustrate how quickly friends can be scared away. Uttering a harsh word or even drawing a sword can be forgiven, if

²⁴The billowing smoke of a furnace
    precedes the fire,
    so insults precede bloodshed.
²⁵I am not ashamed to shelter a
    friend,
    and I will not hide from him.
²⁶But if harm should come to me
    because of him,
all who hear of it will beware of him.

Prayer

²⁷Who will set a guard over my
    mouth,
    an effective seal on my lips,
That I may not fail through them,
    and my tongue may not destroy
    me?

23 ¹Lord, Father and Master of my
    life,
    do not abandon me to their
    designs,
    do not let me fall because of them!

²Who will apply the lash to my
    thoughts,
    and to my mind the rod of disci-
    pline,
That my failings may not be spared
    or the sins of my heart over-
    looked?
³Otherwise my failings may increase,
    and my sins be multiplied;
And I fall before my adversaries,
    and my enemy rejoice over me?
⁴Lord, Father and God of my life,

one seeks reconciliation by apologizing, but a complete betrayal of friendship cannot be mended.

In 22:23 the sage urges support of a friend who is currently poor, for the utilitarian benefit of sharing his future prosperity. Though this advice may appear self-serving, it reflects the belief that God rewards good actions (17:22-23). Ben Sira's insistence on fidelity contrasts with the attitude of the fair-weather friend (6:10-11). Despite the widespread shunning of the poor (Prov 19:4, 7), the sage insists that it is no shame to help a friend who needs support (Lev 25:35-36).

22:27–23:27 Control of the tongue and the passions

This poem comprises a double prayer for discipline of the tongue and of the passions (22:27–23:6), plus instruction on controlling the tongue (23:7-15) and the passions (23:16-27). The need for divine help to guard one's mouth echoes Psalm 141:3. In 23:1 (as in 23:4) the sage addresses God as Father (51:10), a rare divine title in the Hebrew Bible (Isa 63:16; Mal 2:10). Calling God Father is more common in Hellenistic Judaism (Wis 2:16; 14:3) and is Jesus' standard address to God (Luke 11:2; Mark 14:36). In 23:2 the sage recognizes that he needs the "rod of discipline" (Prov 22:15; Ps 141:5) to save him from uncontrolled thoughts and desires, which if unchecked would lead him into sinful shame.

After his prayer, the sage offers teaching on control of the tongue (23:7-15). He urges avoidance of uttering God's holy name in oaths (Exod 20:7;

do not give me haughty eyes;
⁵remove evil desire from my
      heart.
⁶Let neither gluttony nor lust over-
      come me;
do not give me up to shameless
      desires.

Proper Use of the Tongue

⁷Listen, my children, to instruction
      concerning the mouth,
for whoever keeps it will not be
      ensnared.
⁸Through the lips the sinner is
      caught;
by them the reviler and the arro-
      gant are tripped up.

⁹Do not accustom your mouth to
      oaths,
or habitually utter the Holy Name.
¹⁰Just as a servant constantly under
      scrutiny
will not be without bruises,
So one who swears continually by
      the Holy Name
will never remain free from sin.
¹¹Those who swear many oaths heap
      up offenses;
and the scourge will never be far
      from their houses.
If they swear in error, guilt is
      incurred;
if they neglect their obligation,
      the sin is doubly great.

Deut 5:11), which are often an occasion of sin. According to 23:11, there is a danger of a double sin: initially making a rash oath, and then failing to fulfill it (Lev 5:4; Num 30:2). According to some biblical law codes (Lev 24:15-16; John 10:33), blasphemy merits death. Students who forget to discipline their tongue while sitting among the mighty will end up saying something offensive from habit, and will then wish they had never been born (Job 3:3; Jer 20:14) because of the resulting shame to themselves and their family.

In 23:16-27 the sage warns against lack of control of physical passion on the part of a man (23:16-21) or a woman (23:22-26). Ben Sira seems to distinguish between three kinds of male sin (23:16-17). The first is fornication with an unmarried woman, a passion whose fire can be destructive (1 Cor 7:9). The second kind of sin is a sexual relationship with a close relative, as forbidden in the law of Moses (Lev 18:6), a sin that can bring the fire of the divine displeasure (Num 11:1). The third kind of sin, adultery with a married woman (9:9), is like pleasant bread eaten in secret (Prov 9:17; 30:20), but ends in death (Prov 7:22-27).

Sirach 23:18-21 develops the scenario of the third case. Like the sinner in 16:20-21, the adulterer thinks that God will take no notice of him (Job 24:15; Isa 29:15). Yet in fact God is aware of all human activity (17:19-20), even when it is hidden from others (Prov 5:21). Like 42:18, 23:20 asserts that

If they swear without reason they
cannot be declared innocent,
for their households will be filled
with calamities.

¹²There are words comparable to
death;
may they never be heard in the
inheritance of Jacob.
To the devout all such words are
foreign;
they do not wallow in sin.
¹³Do not accustom your mouth to
coarse talk,
for it involves sinful speech.
¹⁴Keep your father and mother in
mind
when you sit among the mighty,
Lest you forget yourself in their
presence
and disgrace your upbringing.
Then you will wish you had never
been born
and will curse the day of your
birth.

¹⁵Those accustomed to using abusive language
will never acquire discipline as
long as they live.

Sins of the Flesh

¹⁶Two types of people multiply sins,
and a third draws down wrath:
Burning passion is like a blazing fire,
not to be quenched till it burns
itself out;
One unchaste with his kindred
never stops until fire breaks forth.
¹⁷To the unchaste all bread is sweet;
he is never through till he dies.

¹⁸The man who dishonors his
marriage bed
says to himself, "Who can see me?
Darkness surrounds me, walls hide
me,
no one sees me. Who can stop
me from sinning?"
He is not mindful of the Most High,
¹⁹fearing only human eyes.

God has advance knowledge of what will happen (Ps 139:1-6). According to 23:21, the unsuspecting adulterer will not escape public punishment (Prov 6:32-35). Indeed, the Torah commanded death by stoning (Lev 20:10; Deut 22:21), although later Jewish law practically eliminated this punishment.

Ben Sira then warns of the evils of a woman's adultery (23:22-27). Her offense is threefold: first, breaking the divine law (Deut 5:18; Exod 20:14); second, acting unjustly against her husband; and third, bearing children fathered by another man. The adulterous woman will suffer the public punishment of stoning to death (Deut 22:22; Dan 13:36-41), while her hope of numerous successful children and grandchildren will be brought to nothing (Wis 3:16-19; 4:3-6). Instead of leaving a good name behind her, her memory will be a disgrace (41:5-9). Meditating on the fate of the virtuous and sinners will convince the student that there is nothing better in life than fearing God (25:10-11; 40:26-27) and keeping God's commands (Eccl 12:13; Deut 10:12-13).

He does not realize that the eyes of
the Lord,
ten thousand times brighter than
the sun,
Observe every step taken
and peer into hidden corners.
²⁰The one who knows all things
before they exist
still knows them all after they
are made.
²¹Such a man will be denounced in
the streets of the city;
and where he least suspects it,
he will be apprehended.

²²So it is with the woman unfaithful
to her husband,
who offers him an heir by
another man.
²³First of all, she has disobeyed the
law of the Most High;
second, she has wronged her
husband;
Third, through her wanton adultery
she has brought forth children by
another man.
²⁴Such a woman will be dragged
before the assembly,

and her punishment will extend
to her children.
²⁵Her children will not take root;
her branches will not bring forth
fruit.

²⁶She will leave behind an accursed
memory;
her disgrace will never be blotted
out.
²⁷Thus all who dwell on the earth
shall know,
all who remain in the world shall
understand,
That nothing is better than the fear
of the Lord,
nothing sweeter than obeying
the commandments of
the Lord.

Praise of Wisdom

24 ¹Wisdom sings her own praises,
among her own people she proclaims her glory.
²In the assembly of the Most High
she opens her mouth,
in the presence of his host she
tells of her glory:

WISDOM IN DOMESTIC LIFE

Sirach 24:1–32:13

24:1-33 The praise of wisdom

Like Proverbs 8:22-36, this poem is an important witness to Israel's
developing theology of wisdom. According to Proverbs 8:22, wisdom came
into being as the first of God's works and was present at the creation. Like
Baruch 3:37–4:1, Ben Sira specifies that wisdom is found in the law of Moses
(24:23). Christian theology has equated wisdom with Christ (1 Cor 1:30).
In Catholic piety, the female figure of wisdom in Sirach 24 has also been
applied to Mary, seen as "Seat of Wisdom."

Sirach 24:1-2 sets the scene for wisdom's speech to God's people on
earth and the heavenly hosts. Although wisdom's first-person declaration

³"From the mouth of the Most High
 I came forth,
 and covered the earth like a mist.
⁴In the heights of heaven I dwelt,
 and my throne was in a pillar of
 cloud.
⁵The vault of heaven I compassed
 alone,
 and walked through the deep
 abyss.
⁶Over waves of the sea, over all the
 land,
 over every people and nation I
 held sway.
⁷Among all these I sought a resting
 place.
 In whose inheritance should I
 abide?

⁸"Then the Creator of all gave me
 his command,
 and my Creator chose the spot
 for my tent.
He said, 'In Jacob make your dwelling,
 in Israel your inheritance.'
⁹Before all ages, from the beginning,
 he created me,
 and through all ages I shall not
 cease to be.
¹⁰In the holy tent I ministered before
 him,
 and so I was established in Zion.
¹¹In the city he loves as he loves me,
 he gave me rest;
 in Jerusalem, my domain.
¹²I struck root among the glorious
 people,

(24:3-22) draws on Proverbs 8:12-36, there are also parallels in Greek poems praising the goddess Isis. The first part of wisdom's speech (24:3-12) retells Israel's religious history, starting from creation and moving by way of the exodus to the choice of Jerusalem for the temple.

Sirach 24:3 equates wisdom with God's utterance; similarly, John's prologue describes Jesus as the Word (John 1:1). Whereas other biblical texts speak of creation occurring through God's word (Gen 1:3; Ps 33:6) or God's wisdom (Prov 3:19-20; Wis 9:1-2), here the focus is on divine revelation (Prov 2:6). According to 24:3, this wisdom is spread like a mist over the earth (Gen 1:2; 2:6), though her dwelling is in the height of heaven (Bar 3:29). The pillar of cloud was the means of God's saving presence for the Israelites at the time of the exodus (Exod 13:21-22; 14:19-20). Wisdom has a full experience of the height of heaven and the depths of the abyss (Prov 8:24-29; Wis 9:16), as well as control of every nation (Prov 8:15-16).

Despite wisdom's cosmic scope (24:7), she is presented as looking for a home on earth (Bar 3:38). This idea is treated differently in 1 Enoch 42:1-2 (perhaps written during the first century A.D.): "Wisdom went out to dwell with humanity, but she found no dwelling place. Wisdom returned to her place and settled permanently among the angels." In contrast, Ben Sira asserts that the Creator finds her an earthly home, since she is told to pitch her tent among the people of Israel (24:8). Similar imagery occurs in John

in the portion of the Lord, his heritage.

13"Like a cedar in Lebanon I grew tall,
    like a cypress on Mount Hermon;
14I grew tall like a palm tree in Engedi,
    like rosebushes in Jericho;
Like a fair olive tree in the field,
    like a plane tree beside water I grew tall.
15Like cinnamon and fragrant cane,
    like precious myrrh I gave forth perfume;
Like galbanum and onycha and mastic,
    like the odor of incense in the holy tent.

16"I spread out my branches like a terebinth,
    my branches so glorious and so graceful.
17I bud forth delights like a vine;
    my blossoms are glorious and rich fruit.
19Come to me, all who desire me,
    and be filled with my fruits.
20You will remember me as sweeter than honey,
    better to have than the honeycomb.
21Those who eat of me will hunger still,
    those who drink of me will thirst for more.
22Whoever obeys me will not be put to shame,

1:14. Sirach 24:9 states that wisdom was formed from the beginning (Prov 8:22-23) and exists forever (Wis 8:13). She ministered before God like a priest in the "holy tent" or tabernacle in the wilderness after the exodus (Exod 25:8-9), and later came to be established in the temple on Mount Zion. God's love for Jerusalem matches his love for wisdom (Ps 50:2; Prov 8:35), and wisdom holds special authority in the city, because the Torah is its guide (Bar 3:37–4:1). Israel is called the Lord's portion (Deut 32:9), as in 17:17.

Sirach 24:13-14 likens wisdom to six kinds of trees: the majestic Lebanon cedar (1 Kgs 6:9-10), the cypress (2 Kgs 19:23), the palm tree (2 Chr 28:15), the rosebush (Wis 2:8), the olive tree (Judg 9:8), and the plane tree (Ezek 31:8). By comparing wisdom to perfumes and spices, used to make the holy anointing oil and the temple incense (Exod 30:23-38), 24:15 hints at wisdom's priestly attributes. Sirach 24:16-17 then compares wisdom with the terebinth and the vine (Judg 6:11; 9:13). Some later manuscripts include a scribal addition as 24:18.

In 24:19 (as in 6:19 and 51:23) wisdom makes an appeal to her disciples to approach her and receive her fruits (Prov 9:4-6). We may compare Jesus' invitation to come to him for rest (Matt 11:28). Hunger and thirst for divine wisdom will increase the appetite, which will be satisfied only with a further consumption of this food (compare John 6:35). Sirach 24:23 makes a significant theological statement, by connecting wisdom with the covenantal law

"Like a cedar in Lebanon I grew tall, like a cypress on Mount Hermon; I grew tall like a palm tree in Engedi" (Sir 24:13-14).

and those who serve me will
never go astray."

²³All this is the book of the covenant
of the Most High God,
the Law which Moses com-
manded us
as a heritage for the community
of Jacob.
²⁵It overflows, like the Pishon, with
wisdom,
and like the Tigris at the time of
first fruits.
²⁶It runs over, like the Euphrates,
with understanding,
and like the Jordan at harvest
time.
²⁷It floods like the Nile with instruc-
tion,
like the Gihon at vintage time.
²⁸The first human being never
finished comprehending
wisdom,

nor will the last succeed in
fathoming her.
²⁹For deeper than the sea are her
thoughts,
and her counsels, than the great
abyss.

³⁰Now I, like a stream from a river,
and like water channeling into a
garden—
³¹I said, "I will water my plants,
I will drench my flower beds."
Then suddenly this stream of mine
became a river,
and this river of mine became a
sea.
³²Again I will make my teachings
shine forth like the dawn;
I will spread their brightness
afar off.
³³Again I will pour out instruction
like prophecy
and bestow it on generations yet
to come.

---

of Moses (Exod 24:7; Deut 33:4). This linkage occurs elsewhere in Ben Sira
(1:26; 19:20) and in other biblical books (Deut 4:5-6; Bar 4:1).

Ben Sira then compares wisdom's abundant life-giving power to six
famed rivers, four of which are mentioned in the Genesis creation story
(Gen 2:10-14). Though the location of the Pishon is uncertain, the Tigris and
Euphrates are great Mesopotamian rivers (Gen 15:8; Dan 10:4). The Gihon
is either another name for the Nile (Gen 2:13), or a spring in Jerusalem
(1 Kgs 1:38). In 24:28, the first human being who failed to grasp God's
wisdom was Adam (Gen 3:17-19). The latest human being (perhaps the
author) still has not fathomed the divine wisdom, which is deeper than the
abyss (1:3; 43:28).

Sirach 24:30-31 continues the water imagery (Deut 32:2), as the sage
seeks to be a channel for the divine wisdom that offers abundant life (Isa
58:11; Ezek 47:1-12). The sage likens his teaching to light that will shine out
to a great distance from his base in Jerusalem (Isa 2:3-5; Prov 6:23). At the
end of the poem, the Greek adds an extra verse (24:34), almost identical to
33:18, but the New American Bible follows the Syriac by omitting it.

Those Who Are Worthy of Praise

25 ¹With three things I am delighted,
for they are pleasing to the Lord
and to human beings:
Harmony among relatives, friendship among neighbors,
and a wife and a husband living
happily together.
²Three kinds of people I hate,
and I loathe their manner of life:
A proud pauper, a rich liar,
and a lecherous old fool.

³In your youth you did not gather.
How will you find anything in
your old age?
⁴How appropriate is sound judgment
in the gray-haired,
and good counsel in the elderly!

⁵How appropriate is wisdom in the
aged,
understanding and counsel in
the venerable!
⁶The crown of the elderly, wide
experience;
their glory, the fear of the Lord.

⁷There are nine who come to mind
as blessed,
a tenth whom my tongue proclaims:
The man who finds joy in his children,
and the one who lives to see the
downfall of his enemies.
⁸Happy the man who lives with a
sensible woman,

25:1-11 Gifts that bring happiness

More delightful than fraternal harmony and neighborly friendship (Ps 133:1) is a peaceful bond between husband and wife (40:23). More notorious than a proud pauper and a fraudulent magnate is an adulterous old man, since elders were meant to set an example of wisdom for the young (Prov 20:29; Dan 13:5-27). In contrast, Sirach 25:3 advises seeking wisdom in one's youth, while there is still time. The gray hairs of old age are meant to signify the wisdom of experience (Job 12:12), and the greatest glory of the elderly is their God-fearing lifestyle (Prov 16:31; Wis 4:9).

Sirach 25:7-11 describes ten kinds of fortunate people. First comes a parent rejoicing in the gift of children (Ps 127:3-5), then one who sees the downfall of enemies (Ps 112:8). Next the sage notes the happiness of a man dwelling with a sensible wife (Prov 19:14). The yoking together of ox and donkey (Deut 22:10) probably refers to the situation of a man married to two wives (Gen 30:1; 1 Sam 1:6). Sirach 25:8 mentions a person who needs not be ashamed of having spoken unwisely (14:1), nor of having to serve someone considered socially inferior (Eccl 10:5-7; Prov 19:10). The sage also regards as happy someone who has found real friendship (6:14-17), as well as one whose words are listened to (3:29). In conclusion, happy is one who finds wisdom (Prov 4:5-7), but the greatest happiness lies in showing reverence toward God (40:26-27).

and the one who does not plow
with an ox and a donkey
combined.
Happy the one who does not sin
with the tongue,
who does not serve an inferior.
⁹Happy the one who finds a friend,
who speaks to attentive ears.
¹⁰How great is the one who finds
wisdom,
but none is greater than the one
who fears the Lord.
¹¹Fear of the Lord surpasses all else.
To whom can we compare the
one who has it?

Wicked and Virtuous Women

¹³Any wound, but not a wound of
the heart!
Any wickedness, but not the
wickedness of a woman!
¹⁴Any suffering, but not suffering
from one's foes!
Any vengeance, but not the vengeance of one's enemies!
¹⁵There is no poison worse than that
of a serpent,
no venom greater than that of a
woman.
¹⁶I would rather live with a dragon
or a lion

25:13–26:18 Good and bad wives

To the modern Western reader, Ben Sira's view of women appears misogynistic. Despite the praise of the good wife (26:1-4 and 26:13-18), the
main emphasis is on the evil wife (25:12-26; 26:5-12). By advising caution
in relation to women (9:1-9), Ben Sira follows ancient admonitions to young
men. Like Egyptian wisdom literature, the book of Proverbs warns against
foreign women, regarded as a source of temptation for men (Prov 5:1-23;
7:1-27).

Biblical tradition also distinguishes between good and bad wives, as
seen from the male viewpoint. Besides maxims praising a good wife (Prov
12:4; 18:22) and the acrostic poem celebrating the capable woman (Prov
31:10-31), there are also warnings against the quarrelsome wife (Prov 21:9,
19). More than the book of Proverbs, however, Ben Sira focuses on female
faults, perhaps echoing the misogynistic element in eighth- or seventh-
century B.C. Greek writers such as Hesiod and Semonides of Amorgos.

Sirach 25:13 links a wound to the heart with the evil done by a woman,
to express the emotional pain that men can suffer from women, though the
sage ignores the hurt that husbands can cause to their wives. The animal
comparisons of 25:15-17 have a generic resemblance to the way Semonides
likens women to various kinds of animals (*On Women* 1–82). Sirach 25:19
suggests that the sinful man deserves the evil of an unpleasant wife (Eccl
7:26).

In 25:21 Ben Sira warns his young male students not to be led astray by
a woman's beauty or wealth (9:8; 31:6). The inner disposition is important,

than live with a wicked woman. [17]A woman's wicked disposition changes her appearance, and makes her face as dark as a bear. [18]When her husband sits among his neighbors, a bitter sigh escapes him unawares.

[19]There is hardly an evil like that in a woman; may she fall to the lot of the sinner! [20]Like a sandy hill to aged feet is a garrulous wife to a quiet husband.

[21]Do not be enticed by a woman's beauty, or be greedy for her wealth. [22]Harsh is the slavery and great the shame when a wife supports her husband.

[23]Depressed mind, gloomy face, and a wounded heart—a wicked woman. Drooping hands and quaking knees, any wife who does not make her husband happy. [24]With a woman sin had a beginning, and because of her we all die. [25]Allow water no outlet,

---

whereas looks can be deceptive (Prov 11:22; 31:30). According to the patriarchal system of honor, it is shameful when a woman provides her husband's economic support (Tob 2:11-12). In 25:24 the sage asserts that sin's beginning came through a woman (Eve), whose error brought death into the world (Gen 3:1-19; 1 Tim 2:14). Elsewhere, the Bible regards Adam's sin as having introduced death into the world (Rom 5:12-21; 1 Cor 15:22). Ben Sira's portrayal of Eve as the source of the world's troubles may be a distant echo of the Greek legend of Pandora (Hesiod, *Works and Days* 57-104). In 25:25-26 the sage advises his students to divorce an errant wife. The law of Moses allowed divorce if a certificate was given (Deut 24:1-4), though Malachi and Jesus opposed the practice (Mal 2:14-16; Mark 10:2-12).

Ben Sira's discussion of the good wife (26:1-4) praises her for the good she does to her husband. By bringing him long life and joy (Prov 12:4; 18:22), she conveys the blessings promised to the God-fearing person (1:12).

According to 26:5-6, a worse affliction than the slanderous plots of the wicked (51:2-6) is the scourging tongue of a jealous wife in a polygamous marriage. Sirach 26:9 refers to the feminine use of eye make-up as a means of seduction (2 Kgs 9:30; Jer 4:30). For a male in Ben Sira's society, shame was avoided by vigilant control over the female members of the household, whether one's wife or one's daughter (26:10; 42:11). For the modern reader, such an attitude appears an affront to the dignity and freedom of women. According to ancient patriarchal ideology a woman was not unlikely to betray her husband. While the sage speaks obscenely of female lust in 26:12,

and no boldness of speech to a
wicked woman.
²⁶If she does not go along as you
direct,
cut her away from you.

26 ¹Happy the husband of a good
wife;
the number of his days will be
doubled.
²A loyal wife brings joy to her
husband,
and he will finish his years in
peace.
³A good wife is a generous gift
bestowed upon him who fears
the Lord.
⁴Whether rich or poor, his heart is
content,
a smile ever on his face.

⁵There are three things I dread,
and a fourth which terrifies me:
Public slander, the gathering of a
mob,
and false accusation—all harder
to bear than death.
⁶A wife jealous of another wife is
heartache and mourning;
everyone feels the lash of her
tongue.

⁷A wicked wife is a chafing yoke;
taking hold of her is like grasping
a scorpion.

⁸A drunken wife arouses great anger,
for she does not hide her shame.
⁹By her haughty stare and her eye-
lids
an unchaste wife can be recognized.

¹⁰Keep a strict watch over an unruly
wife,
lest, finding an opportunity, she
use it;
¹¹Watch out for her impudent eye,
and do not be surprised if she
betrays you:
¹²As a thirsty traveler opens his
mouth
and drinks from any water
nearby,
So she sits down before every tent
peg
and opens her quiver for every
arrow.

¹³A gracious wife delights her
husband;
her thoughtfulness puts flesh on
his bones.
¹⁴A silent wife is a gift from the Lord;
nothing is worth more than her
self-discipline.
¹⁵A modest wife is a supreme blessing;
no scales can weigh the worth of
her chastity.

---

he does not condemn the male here, although other parts of the book discuss the faults of men (23:16-21; 25:2).

Sirach 26:13-18 again praises the good wife for her grace, thoughtfulness, and modesty. Indeed, a good wife is more valuable to her husband than all other wealth (36:29). Sirach 26:17-18 uses imagery connected with the temple in Jerusalem (24:10-12; 50:5-11). The beauty of a woman's face is like the light on the *menorah* or lampstand (Exod 25:31-40; 1 Macc 4:49-50), while her legs are as fine as the golden columns of the temple (Exod 26:32; 1 Macc 1:21-23). Some later Greek manuscripts add a further nine verses here, contrasting the devout and the impious wife.

¹⁶The sun rising in the Lord's
heavens—
the beauty of a good wife in her
well-ordered home.
¹⁷The light which shines above the
holy lampstand—
a beautiful face on a stately
figure.
¹⁸Golden columns on silver bases—
so her shapely legs and steady
feet.

Dangers to Integrity and Friendship

²⁸Two things bring grief to my heart,
and a third arouses my anger:
The wealthy reduced to want,
the intelligent held in contempt,

And those who pass from
righteousness to sin—
the Lord prepares them for the
sword.

²⁹A merchant can hardly keep from
wrongdoing,
nor can a shopkeeper stay free
from sin;

27 ¹For the sake of profit many sin,
and the struggle for wealth
blinds the eyes.
²A stake will be driven between
fitted stones—
sin will be wedged in between
buying and selling.

26:28–27:15 Warning about sinful persons

The opening numerical saying outlines affronts to the proper order of things, such as the scandal of a righteous person turning to sin (Ezek 18:24). The sage then speaks of the sinfulness that can accompany business ventures (26:29–27:3). A merchant cannot easily remain faultless because of the temptation to dishonesty and the desire to increase profits (Amos 8:4-6; Lev 19:35-36). Love of money can cause many to sin (Prov 28:20; 1 Tim 6:10). A house is built up by God-fearing behavior but destroyed by ungodliness (Prov 12:7; 14:11). Speech tests a person's character (27:4-7), like a sieve that winnows corn or a kiln that fires a potter's jar. Indeed, like the fruit produced by a tree (Luke 6:43-45), speech discloses one's level of self-discipline.

Sirach 27:8-15 contrasts the wise and the foolish. The sage exhorts his students to pursue righteousness (Deut 16:20) so that it becomes their glorious clothing (Isa 61:10; Job 29:14). However, the quest for an upright life cannot be undertaken in isolation (27:9), and indeed "birds of a feather flock together." Whereas the bird is an image for fidelity, the lion symbolizes predatory behavior (21:2), namely, the attack of sin on evildoers (Gen 4:7). Sirach 27:11 praises the consistent wisdom of the devout (5:10-11). Understanding is learned through spending time with wise persons (9:14-16), whereas time spent with a fool brings no insights (22:12). The wicked are known for their offensive talk, callous laughter, wrangling, and cursing (Gal 5:19-21).

³Unless one holds fast to the fear of the Lord,
    with sudden swiftness will one's house be thrown down.

⁴When a sieve is shaken, the husks appear;
    so do people's faults when they speak.
⁵The furnace tests the potter's vessels;
    the test of a person is in conversation.
⁶The fruit of a tree shows the care it has had;
    so speech discloses the bent of a person's heart.
⁷Praise no one before he speaks,
    for it is then that people are tested.
⁸If you strive after justice, you will attain it,
    and wear it like a splendid robe.
⁹Birds nest with their own kind,
    and honesty comes to those who work at it.
¹⁰A lion lies in wait for prey,
    so does sin for evildoers.

¹¹The conversation of the godly is always wisdom,
    but the fool changes like the moon.
¹²Limit the time you spend among the stupid,
    but frequent the company of the thoughtful.
¹³The conversation of fools is offensive,
    and their laughter is wanton sin.
¹⁴Their oath-filled talk makes the hair stand on end,
    and their brawls make one stop the ears.
¹⁵The wrangling of the proud ends in bloodshed,
    and their cursing is painful to hear.

¹⁶Whoever betrays a secret destroys confidence,
    and will never find a congenial friend.
¹⁷Cherish your friend, keep faith with him;
    but if you betray his secrets, do not go after him;

27:16–28:7 Avoiding anger

According to 27:16-21, breaking confidences will destroy a friendship (Prov 11:13; 25:9), whereas fidelity will build up a friendly relationship (6:14-17). A friend whose secrets have been disclosed will disappear, just as a bird flies away (22:20) or a gazelle runs from a trap (Prov 6:5). Whereas a friend's hurtful action or abusive talk can be forgiven, revealing secrets will cause the irretrievable breakdown of the friendship (22:22).

Next (27:22-27), the sage advises against associating with evil people (Prov 6:12-15; 1 Cor 15:33). As in 12:16, he warns of the hidden malice of flatterers (Prov 26:24-26). In 27:24 he reveals his own feeling of hatred of such deceitful people, perhaps because they nearly caused his death by denouncing him (51:2-6). As in 12:6, Ben Sira asserts God's hatred of sinners (Prov 6:16-19). Then 27:25-27 provides a reminder of the belief that God will punish evildoers in this life (Prov 6:15). Since those who dig a hole to

18For as one might kill another,
  you have killed your neighbor's
    friendship.
19Like a bird released from your
    hand,
  you have let your friend go and
    cannot recapture him.
20Do not go after him, for he is far
    away,
  and has escaped like a gazelle
    from a snare.
21For a wound can be bandaged,
  and an insult forgiven,
  but whoever betrays secrets
    does hopeless damage.

Malice, Anger and Vengeance

22Whoever has shifty eyes plots
    mischief
  and those who know him will
    keep their distance;
23In your presence he uses honeyed
    talk,
  and admires your words,

But later he changes his tone
  and twists the words to your ruin.
24I have hated many things but not
    as much as him,
  and the Lord hates him as well.
25A stone falls back on the head of
    the one who throws it high,
  and a treacherous blow causes
    many wounds.
26Whoever digs a pit falls into it,
  and whoever lays a snare is
    caught in it.
27The evil anyone does will recoil
    on him
  without knowing how it came
    upon him.

28Mockery and abuse will befall the
    arrogant,
  and vengeance lies in wait for
    them like a lion.
29Those who rejoice in the downfall
    of the godly will be caught in
    a snare,

trap others will fall in it themselves (Prov 26:27), the way to escape receiving evil is to refrain from doing evil (7:1-3).

Sirach 27:28–28:1 consists of warnings against vengefulness. Those who delight in setting traps will be ensnared in them, thereby suffering pain (Ps 7:15-17). The retribution mentioned in 27:29 finds an illustration in the punishment of Haman (Esth 7:10). Those who take vengeance into their own hands will become victims of divine vengeance (Deut 32:35; Rom 12:19).

Sirach 28:2-7 approaches the tone of Jesus' teaching on forgiveness. Pardoning others is a condition for receiving divine forgiveness (Mark 11:25), whereas refusing mercy to someone else makes it unreasonable to expect mercy from the Lord (Matt 18:23-35). If God forgives offenses (17:29), human beings would do well to act similarly (Luke 6:36-37). The thought of death should turn people away from enmity, since in Ben Sira's view sins are punished before death (7:36; 11:26-28). By remembering the commandment to love one's neighbor as oneself (Lev 19:18), a person will be led to overlook the failings of others.

and pain will consume them before they die.
³⁰Wrath and anger, these also are
abominations,
yet a sinner holds on to them.

28 ¹The vengeful will face the
Lord's vengeance;
indeed he remembers their sins
in detail.

²Forgive your neighbor the wrong
done to you;
then when you pray, your own
sins will be forgiven.
³Does anyone nourish anger against
another
and expect healing from the
LORD?
⁴Can one refuse mercy to a sinner
like oneself,
yet seek pardon for one's own
sins?
⁵If a mere mortal cherishes wrath,
who will forgive his sins?
⁶Remember your last days and set
enmity aside;
remember death and decay, and
cease from sin!
⁷Remember the commandments
and do not be angry with
your neighbor;

remember the covenant of the
Most High, and overlook
faults.

⁸Avoid strife and your sins will be
fewer,
for the hot-tempered kindle strife;
⁹The sinner disrupts friendships
and sows discord among those
who are at peace.
¹⁰The more the wood, the greater
the fire,
the more the cruelty, the fiercer
the strife;
The greater the strength, the sterner
the anger,
the greater the wealth, the
greater the wrath.
¹¹Pitch and resin make fire flare up,
and a hasty quarrel provokes
bloodshed.

The Evil Tongue

¹²If you blow on a spark, it turns
into flame,
if you spit on it, it dies out;
yet both you do with your mouth!
¹³Cursed be gossips and the double-
tongued,
for they destroy the peace of
many.

28:8-26 Quarrelsomeness and evils of the tongue

One way to avoid sinning is to keep away from disputes, since the quarrelsome person will disrupt friendships (Prov 15:18; 16:28). Quarrelers add fuel to the fire (Prov 26:20-21; Jas 3:5-6), particularly if they are rich and powerful (8:1-3; 13:2), and the resulting arguments can even lead to bloodshed (22:24; 27:15). According to 28:12, the same mouth has power either to kindle argument (11:32) or to extinguish it (Prov 15:1; 18:21). A false accusation might even cause an innocent wife to be divorced by her husband.

Sirach 28:17 notes that the tongue can be very hurtful (Prov 25:15; Jas 3:5-8). The burden imposed by slander is as heavy as the iron yoke of

¹⁴A meddlesome tongue subverts
many,
and makes them refugees among
peoples.
It destroys strong cities,
and overthrows the houses of
the great.
¹⁵A meddlesome tongue drives
virtuous women from their
homes,
and robs them of the fruit of
their toil.
¹⁶Whoever heed it will find no rest,
nor will they dwell in peace.

¹⁷A blow from a whip raises a welt,
but a blow from the tongue will
break bones.
¹⁸Many have fallen by the edge of
the sword,
but not as many as by the tongue.
¹⁹Happy the one who is sheltered
from it,
and has not endured its wrath;
Who has not borne its yoke
nor been bound with its chains.
²⁰For its yoke is a yoke of iron,
and its chains are chains of
bronze;
²¹The death it inflicts is an evil death,
even Sheol is preferable to it.

²²It will have no power over the
godly,
nor will they be burned in its
flame.
²³But those who forsake the Lord
will fall victim to it,
as it burns among them un-
quenchably;
It will hurl itself against them like a
lion,
and like a leopard, it will tear
them to pieces.
²⁴As you fence in your property
with thorns,
so make a door and a bolt for
your mouth.
²⁵As you lock up your silver and
gold,
so make balances and scales for
your words.
²⁶Take care not to slip by your tongue
and fall victim to one lying in
ambush.

Loans, Alms and Surety

29 ¹The merciful lend to their
neighbor,
by holding out a helping hand,
they keep the command-
ments.

Nebuchadnezzar's conquest of Judah (Jer 28:13-14). Slander can make life not worth living (26:5). Because of divine deliverance (51:3-4), the fire kindled by slanderers will ultimately harm the godless but not the just (Isa 43:2; 66:24). According to 28:24, just as a farmer protects his property with a hedge (Isa 5:2), so the wise need to guard their mouths from slander. As a banker weighs and seals moneybags (Job 14:16-17), so sensible students weigh their words and seal their lips (21:25; 22:27). Careless persons, tripped up by their tongues, will fall victim to the onlookers (Prov 13:3; 21:23).

29:1-20 Loans, donations, and guarantees

According to 29:1, it is a kindness to lend to a needy neighbor without demanding interest (Exod 22:24; Lev 25:35-37). Unlike the scoundrel (Ps 37:21),

²Lend to your neighbor in his time of need,
and pay back your neighbor in time.
³Keep your promise and be honest with him,
and at all times you will find what you need.
⁴Many borrowers ask for a loan
and cause trouble for those who help them.
⁵Till he gets a loan, he kisses the lender's hand
and speaks softly of his creditor's money,
But at time of payment, delays,
makes excuses, and finds fault with the timing.
⁶If he can pay, the lender will recover barely half,
and will consider that a windfall.
If he cannot pay, the lender is cheated of his money
and acquires an enemy at no extra charge;
With curses and insults the borrower will repay,
and instead of honor will repay with abuse.
⁷Many refuse to lend, not out of meanness,
but from fear of being cheated needlessly.

⁸But with those in humble circumstances be patient;
do not keep them waiting for your alms.
⁹Because of the commandment, help the poor,
and in their need, do not send them away empty-handed.
¹⁰Lose your money for relative or friend;
do not hide it under a stone to rot.

---

the honest borrower keeps faith with the promise made, by repaying a loan at the required time. Sirach 29:4-6 outlines the common troubles of lenders; far from receiving gratitude, they often suffer grief from the borrowers. Before receiving a loan, the applicant is full of flattery, but when the money is due, the only repayment will be excuses. Even if the debtor can afford to repay, the creditor will be pleased to recover half the loan (8:12), whereas if the debtor cannot afford repayment, the creditor has lost the money and also gained an enemy for no extra cost! If the debtor does repay, it will be with curses rather than with gratitude. Often prudence rather than meanness leads people to refuse to lend.

In case the observations of 29:4-7 seem harsh, 29:8-13 encourages charitable donations. As in 4:1-4, the sage urges helping the poor without delay (Prov 3:28), because the Torah commands offering generous assistance (Deut 15:7-8; Ps 112:5). Instead of leaving money to rot (Matt 6:19; Jas 5:2-3), it is better to use it for the benefit of relatives and friends (14:13). According to 29:11-13 and 40:24, charitable giving will provide deliverance from evil (Prov 19:17; Tob 12:9).

¹¹Dispose of your treasure according to the commandments of the Most High, and that will profit you more than the gold.
¹²Store up almsgiving in your treasury, and it will save you from every evil.
¹³Better than a mighty shield and a sturdy spear it will fight for you against the enemy.

¹⁴A good person will be surety for a neighbor, but whoever has lost a sense of shame will fail him.
¹⁵Do not forget the kindness of your backer, for he has given his very life for you.
¹⁶A sinner will turn the favor of a pledge into misfortune, ¹⁷and the ungrateful will abandon his rescuer.
¹⁸Going surety has ruined many who were prosperous and tossed them about like waves of the sea; It has exiled the prominent and sent them wandering through foreign lands.
¹⁹The sinner will come to grief through surety, and whoever undertakes too much will fall into lawsuits.
²⁰Help your neighbor according to your means, but take care lest you fall yourself.

Frugality and Its Rewards

²¹Life's prime needs are water, bread, and clothing, and also a house for decent privacy.

Sirach 29:14-20 speaks of the dangers and benefits of providing collateral guarantees for a neighbor (8:13). A good person will provide the necessary collateral, fully aware of the biblical warnings (Prov 6:1-5; 11:15). The beneficiary of such a guarantee needs to appreciate that the backer has risked his life (Prov 22:26-27), yet the ungrateful person will not acknowledge the help received. Hence, Ben Sira spells out the dangers of providing collateral: financial ruin, and even exile to escape debts. Sirach 29:19 seems to refer to the ambitious guarantor who seeks gain by keeping pledged items such as garments; that person will suffer lawsuits for breaking the rules of the Torah (Exod 22:25; Deut 24:10-13). Hence Ben Sira concludes: be as generous as you can, but also have a prudent regard for your own welfare (Tob 4:8).

29:21–30:13 Household management

Sirach 29:21-28 concerns self-sufficiency. Whereas 39:26 lists ten necessities for life, 29:21 picks out three of them (water, bread, and clothing), and adds housing. While the Stoic philosophers praised self-sufficiency, the aphorism of 29:22 also has biblical parallels (Prov 12:9; 17:1). Sirach 29:23-24

²²Better is the life of the poor under
the shadow of their own roof
than sumptuous banquets among
strangers.
²³Whether little or much, be content
with what you have:
then you will hear no reproach
as a parasite.
²⁴It is a miserable life to go from
house to house,
for where you are a guest you
dare not open your
mouth.
²⁵You will entertain and provide
drink without being thanked;
besides, you will hear these bitter
words:
²⁶"Come here, you parasite, set the
table,
let me eat the food you have
there!
²⁷Go away, you parasite, for one
more worthy;

for my relative's visit I need the
room!"
²⁸Painful things to a sensitive person
are rebuke as a parasite and
insults from creditors.

The Training of Children

30 ¹Whoever loves a son will
chastise him often,
that he may be his joy when he
grows up.
²Whoever disciplines a son will
benefit from him,
and boast of him among
acquaintances.
³Whoever educates a son will make
his enemy jealous,
and rejoice in him among his
friends.
⁴At the father's death, he will seem
not dead,
for he leaves after him one like
himself,

---

calls on the wise person to be content with a few basic needs (Prov 30:8;
1 Tim 6:8), since it is miserable to always be the guest of other people (Prov
27:8; 2 Kgs 8:1). The visitor is treated like a slave, being told to serve food
(Luke 17:8), and moved to an inferior place to accommodate visiting relatives (29:25-27). For the self-respecting student of wisdom, it is painful to
be dependent on others for hospitality.

Sirach 30:1-13 deals with the disciplining of sons. The hoped-for benefit
of discipline is subsequent good behavior (Prov 10:1; 22:6) that will bring
joy to the child's parents (25:7). Indeed, the disciplined son is a worthy
replacement for his father (Tob 9:6), in a society esteeming conformity to
patriarchal models. Lacking a clear idea of an afterlife (14:16; 17:27-28), Ben
Sira considered it important for a male to perpetuate his name by fathering
a dutiful son (40:19), as well as by leaving behind a good reputation (41:13;
44:8). Sirach 30:6 sees the son's role as avenging insults offered to his father
(Ps 127:5), as well as rewarding kindnesses (1 Kgs 2:7). Ben Sira then warns
against pampering a son. The spoiled child foolishly incurs wounds (or
inflicts them on others), leaving the father to bandage them. A child needs
discipline (Prov 29:15), just as a horse has to be broken in (Prov 26:3). Ac-

⁵Whom he looked upon through
life with joy,
and in death, without regret.
⁶Against his enemies he has left an
avenger,
and one to repay his friends with
kindness.

⁷Whoever spoils a son will have
wounds to bandage,
and will suffer heartache at every
cry.
⁸An untamed horse turns out stubborn;
and a son left to himself grows up
unruly.
⁹Pamper a child and he will be a
terror for you,
indulge him, and he will bring
you grief.
¹⁰Do not laugh with him lest you
share sorrow with him,
and in the end you will gnash
your teeth.
¹¹Do not give him his own way in
his youth,
and do not ignore his follies.

¹²Bow down his head in his youth,
beat his sides while he is still
young,
Lest he become stubborn and disobey you,
and leave you disconsolate.
¹³Discipline your son and make
heavy his yoke,
lest you be offended by his
shamelessness.

Health and Cheerfulness

¹⁴Better the poor in vigorous health
than the rich with bodily ills.
¹⁵I would rather have bodily health
than any gold,
and contentment of spirit than
pearls.
¹⁶No riches are greater than a
healthy body;
and no happiness than a joyful
heart.
¹⁷Better is death than a wretched life,
everlasting sleep than constant
illness.
¹⁸Good things set before one who
cannot eat

---

cording to 30:9, overindulging a child is a disservice that will eventually bring grief. Hence Ben Sira recommends physical punishment (Prov 13:24; 22:15), though his advice seems harsh for modern readers.

30:14–31:11 Physical and material happiness

Sirach 30:14-25 considers the physical happiness produced by good health and an optimistic outlook. Ben Sira sees health as very important (38:1-15). In regarding death as preferable to a bitter life, he echoes feelings voiced by Moses (Num 11:15), Elijah (1 Kgs 19:4), and Job (Job 3:11-13). A meal presented to someone too sick to eat is as useless as the food that pagans offered to the dead (Deut 26:14; Bar 6:26) or to idols (Ps 115:5-6). A hopeful outlook contributes to good health, just as brooding can lead to depression (Prov 15:13; 17:22). Sirach 30:22-25 advocates enjoying the good things in life (Eccl 9:7-9) but leaving aside resentment, envy, and anger, which cause needless distress (28:6-7).

are like food offerings placed
before a tomb.
[19]What good is an offering to an idol
that can neither eat nor smell?
So it is with the one being punished
by the Lord,
[20]who groans at what his eyes
behold.

[21]Do not give in to sadness,
or torment yourself deliberately.
[22]Gladness of heart is the very life
of a person,
and cheerfulness prolongs his
days.
[23]Distract yourself and renew your
courage,
drive resentment far away from
you;
For grief has killed many,
and nothing is to be gained from
resentment.
[24]Envy and anger shorten one's days,
and anxiety brings on premature
old age.
[25]Those who are cheerful and merry
at table
benefit from their food.

The Proper Attitude Toward Riches

31 [1]Wakefulness over wealth wastes
away the flesh,
and anxiety over it drives away
sleep.

[2]Wakeful anxiety banishes slumber;
more than a serious illness it
disturbs repose.
[3]The rich labor to pile up wealth,
and if they rest, it is to enjoy
pleasure;
[4]The poor labor for a meager living,
and if they ever rest, they become
needy.
[5]The lover of gold will not be free
from sin;
whoever pursues money will be
led astray by it.
[6]Many have come to ruin for the
sake of gold,
yet destruction lay before their
very eyes;
[7]It is a stumbling block for fools;
any simpleton will be ensnared
by it.

[8]Happy the rich person found without fault,
who does not turn aside after
wealth.
[9]Who is he, that we may praise him?
For he has done wonders among
his people.
[10]Who has been tested by gold and
been found perfect?
Let it be for him his glory;
Who could have sinned but did not,
and could have done evil but
did not?

Sirach 31:1 notes that the worry of the rich about their money often prevents them from sleeping soundly (Eccl 5:11). Whereas the wealthy can enjoy luxury as a result of their work, the poor labor to survive and cannot afford any rest (40:1-2). The sage points out the moral dangers of wealth (31:5-7) and praises the rich person who has maintained virtue (31:8-11). The corrupting power of unfettered wealth is well known to ethical teachers (Prov 28:20; 1 Tim 6:9-10). Because riches can be a temptation (27:1), anyone who is not led astray by wealth deserves praise (Mark 10:23-25).

11So his good fortune is secure,
and the assembly will recount
his praises.

Table Etiquette

12Are you seated at the table of the
great?
Bring to it no greedy gullet,
Nor say, "How much food there is
here!"
13Remember that the greedy eye
is evil.
What has been created more greedy
than the eye?
Therefore, it weeps for any cause.
15Recognize that your neighbor
feels as you do,
and keep in mind everything
you dislike.

14Toward what he looks at, do not
put out a hand;
nor reach for the same dish
when he does.
16Eat, like anyone else, what is set
before you,
but do not eat greedily, lest you
be despised.
17Be the first to stop, as befits good
manners;
and do not gorge yourself, lest
you give offense.
18If there are many with you at
table,
do not be the first to stretch out
your hand.
19Does not a little suffice for a well-
bred person?

31:12–32:13 Good manners in eating and drinking

While banquets had long been a feature of the life of the oriental ruling classes (Amos 6:4-6; Esth 1:5-9), Greek tradition placed great importance on the banquet and the ensuing drinking party or symposium. Hence Sirach 31:12-21 advocates moderation in eating. Like 14:9-10 and 37:29, Sirach 31:12-13 advises the avoidance of gluttony (Prov 23:1-3), because danger lurks in the greedy eye (Gen 3:6; 1 John 2:16). Ben Sira urges self-restraint in deference to the feelings of others (Lev 19:18; Rom 15:1-2). Dignified behavior entails being the last to reach out for food and the first to stop eating. For disciplined guests, a moderate amount is enough, so that one will avoid the discomfort resulting from excessive consumption. Sirach 31:21 refers to induced vomiting, commonly practiced by wealthy Romans after overeating.

When advocating self-control in drinking (31:22-31), Ben Sira echoes earlier admonitions about the proper consumption of wine, not only from the Bible (Prov 23:29-35; 31:4-7), but also from the writings of the Greek poet Theognis (497–510). Sirach 31:25 warns against competitive drinking (Isa 5:22; Prov 20:1), since intoxication can lead to many evils (Gen 19:31-36; 1 Macc 16:16). For humanity, a moderate consumption of wine enhances life, by contributing to health and joy (Ps 104:15; 1 Tim 5:23), whereas over-indulgence is harmful (31:29-30).

When he lies down, he does not
wheeze.
20Moderate eating ensures sound
slumber
and a clear mind on rising the
next day.
The distress of sleeplessness and of
nausea
and colic are with the glutton!
21Should you have eaten too much,
get up to vomit and you will
have relief.

22Listen to me, my child, and do not
scorn me;
later you will find my advice
good.
In whatever you do, be moderate,
and no sickness will befall you.
23People bless one who is generous
with food,
and this testimony to his goodness is lasting.
24The city complains about one who
is stingy with food,
and this testimony to his stingi-
ness is lasting.
25Let not wine be the proof of your
strength,
for wine has been the ruin of
many.
26As the furnace tests the work of
the smith,

so does wine the hearts of the
insolent.
27Wine is very life to anyone,
if taken in moderation.
Does anyone really live who lacks
the wine
which from the beginning was
created for joy?
28Joy of heart, good cheer, and delight
is wine enough, drunk at the
proper time.
29Headache, bitterness, and disgrace
is wine drunk amid anger and
strife.
30Wine in excess is a snare for the
fool;
it lessens strength and multiplies
wounds.
31Do not wrangle with your neighbor
when wine is served,
nor despise him while he is
having a good time;
Say no harsh words to him
nor distress him by making
demands.

32 1If you are chosen to preside at a
dinner, do not be puffed up,
but with the guests be as one of
them;
Take care of them first and then sit
down;

Ben Sira then outlines good table manners for the banquet presider
(32:1-2), the elders (32:3-6), the younger guests (32:7-10), and all those invited (32:11-13). The person chosen to preside at dinner is to behave humbly
as one of the company (3:17-18), concerned that the guests be satisfied
(2 Macc 2:27). The older guests are entitled to share their wisdom (8:8-9;
25:4-6), if they are careful not to interrupt the musical entertainment. The
younger guests are to wait until the elders invite them to talk (Job 32:6-7),
and then speak briefly. The wise guest also leaves promptly at the proper
time for departing. Above all, the virtuous give thanks to God for the gift
of food and drink (Deut 8:10; John 6:11).

²see to their needs, and then take
your place,
To share in their joy
and receive a wreath for a job
well done.
³You who are older, it is your right
to speak,
but temper your knowledge and
do not interrupt the sing-
ing.
⁴Where there is entertainment, do not
pour out discourse,
and do not display your wisdom
at the wrong time.
⁵Like a seal of carnelian in a setting
of gold:
a concert of music at a banquet
of wine.
⁶A seal of emerald in a work of gold:
the melody of music with deli-
cious wine.
⁷Speak, young man, only when
necessary,
when they have asked you more
than once.
⁸Be brief, say much in few words;
be knowledgeable and yet quiet.
⁹When among elders do not be
forward,

and with officials do not be too
insistent.
¹⁰The lightning that flashes before a
hailstorm:
the esteem that shines on
modesty.
¹¹Leave in good time and do not be
the last;
go home quickly without delay.
¹²There enjoy doing as you wish,
but do not sin through words of
pride.
¹³Above all, bless your Maker,
who showers his favors upon you.

The Providence of God

¹⁴Whoever seeks God must accept
discipline;
and whoever resorts to him
obtains an answer.
¹⁵Whoever seeks the law will master
it,
but the hypocrite will be ensnared
by it.
¹⁶Whoever fears the LORD will understand what is right,
and out of obscurity he will draw
forth a course of action.
¹⁷The lawless turn aside warnings

USING WISDOM TO MAKE GOOD DECISIONS

Sirach 32:14–38:23

32:14–33:18 Divine providence

Whereas the honest seeker for God is enlightened through study of the law of Moses (32:14-16), sinners reject correction. Sirach 32:18 declares that the sensible person heeds the advice rejected by the arrogant (Prov 12:15; Tob 4:18). According to 32:24, observance of the Torah leads to self-preservation (Prov 19:16). Sirach 33:1-3 contrasts the consistent God-fearing person with unstable apostates, who are tossed about like a ship in a tempest (Jonah 1:5; Eph 4:14). For the wise, God's word is as reliable as the priestly oracle given through the sacred lots of Urim and Thummim (Exod 28:30; Num 27:21).

and distort the law to suit their purpose.

¹⁸The sensible will not neglect direction;
the proud and insolent are deterred by no fear.
¹⁹Do nothing without deliberation;
then once you have acted, have no regrets.
²⁰Do not go on a way set with snares,
and do not stumble on the same thing twice.
²¹Do not trust the road, because of bandits;
²²be careful on your paths.
²³Whatever you do, be on your guard,
for whoever does so keeps the commandments.
²⁴Whoever keeps the law preserves himself;
and whoever trusts in the LORD shall not be put to shame.

33 ¹No evil can harm the one who fears the LORD;
through trials, again and again he is rescued.
²Whoever hates the law is without wisdom,
and is tossed about like a boat in a storm.
³The prudent trust in the word of the LORD,
and the law is dependable for them as a divine oracle.
⁴Prepare your words and then you will be listened to;
draw upon your training, and give your answer.

⁵Like the wheel of a cart is the mind of a fool,
and his thoughts like a turning axle.
⁶A mocking friend is like a stallion that neighs, no matter who the rider may be.

Having contrasted wise and foolish persons, Ben Sira investigates why the world contains both good and evil people (33:7-15). The sage first considers God's allocation of times (Eccl 3:1-8; Dan 2:21), as seen in the Jewish religious calendar. While in principle every day is of equal value, God has selected some to be special. Days such as sabbaths and festivals are holy (Gen 2:3; Lev 23:2), but other days are ordinary (Rom 14:5; 2 Tim 2:20). So, too, people differ because God has decreed their differing paths (33:10-11). God is like a potter, shaping human beings according to the divine will (Isa 29:16; Rom 9:21). In 33:12 Ben Sira implies that the Israelites are the chosen people whom God has blessed and made holy (Gen 12:2; Exod 19:6). By contrast (according to 16:9), those cursed and dispossessed include the Canaanites (Deut 7:1-2), but the idea of a divine curse on people raises many questions for modern readers of the Bible.

In Ben Sira's scheme here (33:13), God's decree assigns good and evil in a rather deterministic way, as in the Qumran Community Rule (1QS 3:15-4:1). Ben Sira's theodicy is based on a system of paired opposites (42:24-25), such as good and evil (Job 2:10; Eccl 7:13-14; Isa 45:7). Sirach 33:14-15

⁷Why is one day more important
than another,
when the same sun lights up
every day of the year?
⁸By the LORD's knowledge they are
kept distinct;
and he designates the seasons
and feasts.
⁹Some he exalts and sanctifies,
and others he lists as ordinary
days.
¹⁰Likewise, all people are of clay,
and from earth humankind was
formed;
¹¹In the fullness of his knowledge
the Lord distinguished them,
and he designated their different
ways.
¹²Some he blessed and exalted,
and some he sanctified and drew
to himself.
Others he cursed and brought low,
and expelled them from their
place.
¹³Like clay in the hands of a potter,
to be molded according to his
pleasure,

So are people in the hands of their
Maker,
to be dealt with as he decides.
¹⁴As evil contrasts with good, and
death with life,
so are sinners in contrast with
the godly.
¹⁵See now all the works of the Most
High:
they come in pairs, one the
opposite of the other.

¹⁶Now I am the last to keep vigil,
like a gleaner following the
grape-pickers;
¹⁷Since by the Lord's blessing I have
made progress
till like a grape-picker I have
filled my wine press,
¹⁸Consider that not for myself only
have I labored,
but for all who seek instruction.

Property and Servants

¹⁹Listen to me, leaders of the
people;
rulers of the congregation, pay
heed!

---

may be echoing the Stoic philosopher Chrysippus (d. ca. 206 B.C.): "Since goods are opposite to evils, the two must necessarily exist in opposition to each other" (*On Providence*, fragment 1169).

In 33:16-18, Ben Sira concludes this poem on a personal note (24:30-33; 34:12-13), comparing himself to a gleaner following the grape pickers (Lev 19:10; Deut 24:21). His toil has not been simply for his own benefit, but to help everyone seeking wisdom (51:23-28).

33:19–33 Property and servants

Ben Sira's cautious advice is to retain patriarchal control of household power as long as possible (33:20-23), so as to avoid the shame of depending on others for one's livelihood (29:24-28; 40:28-30). Sirach 33:24 even suggests waiting until one's deathbed before distributing property to the heirs (Tob 4:1-2).

20aLet neither son nor wife, neither brother nor friend,
   have power over you as long as you live.
21While breath of life is still in you,
   let no one take your place.
20bDo not give your wealth to another,
   lest you must plead for support yourself.
22Far better that your children plead with you
   than that you should look for a handout from them.
23Keep control over all your affairs;
   bring no stain on your honor.

24When your few days reach their limit,
   at the time of death distribute your inheritance.
25Fodder and whip and loads for a donkey;
   food, correction and work for a slave.
26Make a slave work, and he will look for rest;
   let his hands be idle and he will seek to be free.
27The yoke and harness will bow the neck;
   and for a wicked slave, punishment in the stocks.

Sirach 33:25-33 discusses treatment of slaves, regarded in the ancient world as their masters' property (Deut 5:21). The first part (33:25-30) enjoins harsh treatment, whereas the second part (33:31-33) urges kindness. The saying of 33:25, based on Proverbs 26:3, makes the demeaning comparison of a slave to a beast of burden. Slaves who are forced to work will only look for their rest, but those left idle will seek freedom (Exod 5:4, 17). Sirach 33:27 advocates physical punishment for recalcitrant slaves (Prov 29:19), even confining them in the stocks (Jer 20:2). By contrast, the New Testament letters teach that slaves be treated humanely (Eph 6:9; Col 4:1). Sirach 33:28 warns against leaving slaves unoccupied (Prov 21:25), while 33:30 advises loading the unruly slave with heavy metal fetters (Lam 3:7). Nevertheless, the sage urges the student not to impose his superiority over others, and to do nothing unjust against the law of Moses. In fact, the Torah protected what limited rights slaves had (Exod 21:1-11; Deut 15:12-18).

Ben Sira now echoes the Torah in urging kind treatment for a reliable household slave (33:31-33), who is to be treated like oneself (Exod 21:5-6; Lev 19:18) and regarded as one of the family (7:21). Indeed, treating such a slave like a brother fulfils the Torah (Lev 25:39-40), which urges generous treatment of an impoverished compatriot. Apart from prisoners of war (1 Macc 8:10-11), many slaves were fellow Israelites who had fallen into debt (Prov 11:29). Ben Sira concludes that if such a slave runs away, he is lost forever, since the Torah forbids returning a runaway slave to his master (Deut 23:16-17).

²⁸Force him to work that he be not
idle,
²⁹for idleness teaches much mischief.
³⁰Put him to work, as is fitting for
him;
and if he does not obey, load
him with chains.
But never lord it over any human
being,
and do nothing unjust.
³¹If you have but one slave, treat
him like yourself,
for you have acquired him with
your life's blood;
If you have but one slave, deal with
him as a brother,
for you need him as you need
your life.
³²If you mistreat him and he runs
away,
³³in what direction will you look
for him?

Trust in the Lord and Not in Dreams

34 ¹Empty and false are the hopes
of the senseless,
and dreams give wings to fools.
²Like one grasping at shadows or
chasing the wind,
so anyone who believes in
dreams.
³What is seen in dreams is a reflec-
tion,
the likeness of a face looking at
itself.
⁴How can the unclean produce what
is clean?
How can the false produce what
is true?
⁵Divination, omens, and dreams are
unreal;
what you already expect, the
mind fantasizes.
⁶Unless they are specially sent by
the Most High,
do not fix your heart on them.

34:1-20 Devout wisdom more reliable than dreams

This poem has three sections: the futility of dreams (34:1-8); the value
of wisdom amid life's experiences (34:9-13); and the benefit of fear of the
Lord (34:14-20). The ancient Greeks often thought dreams carried messages
from the gods (Plato, *Crito* 44a), while Jewish apocalyptic texts told of
Enoch's dream visions (1 Enoch 13:10; 83:3). By contrast, Ben Sira adopts
the Deuteronomic suspicion of dreams as leading people away from the
one true God (Deut 13:2-5; Jer 23:25-32). Trusting in dreams is like chasing
the wind (Eccl 5:2). Ben Sira generally links dreams with divinations and
omens, which the Torah forbids (Lev 19:26; Deut 18:10-14). However, dreams
can be sent by God, as happened to Joseph, Solomon, and Eliphaz (Gen
37:5-10; 1 Kgs 3:5-15; Job 4:12-21). Whereas false dreams have led many
astray (Jer 29:8-9), perfect wisdom can be reliably found in the law of Moses.
Sirach 34:9-13 speaks of the wisdom gained through travel (39:4). The
understanding that Ben Sira gained on his journeys (possibly to Alexandria)
may have included some acquaintance with Greek or Egyptian literature.
Another source of wisdom is the testing experience of travel hazards (2 Cor
11:25-26).

⁷For dreams have led many astray,
 and those who put their hope in
 them have perished.
⁸Without such deceptions the Law
 will be fulfilled,
 and in the mouth of the faithful
 is complete wisdom.

⁹A much-traveled person knows
 many things;
 and one with much experience
 speaks sense.
¹⁰An inexperienced person knows
 little,
 ¹¹whereas with travel one adds
 to resourcefulness.
¹²I have seen much in my travels,
 and learned more than I could
 ever say.
¹³Often I was in danger of death,
 but by these experiences I was
 saved.

¹⁴Living is the spirit of those who
 fear the Lord,
 ¹⁵for their hope is in their savior.
¹⁶Whoever fear the Lord are afraid
 of nothing
 and are never discouraged, for
 he is their hope.
¹⁷Happy the soul that fears the Lord!

¹⁸In whom does he trust, and
 who is his support?
¹⁹The eyes of the Lord are upon those
 who love him;
 he is their mighty shield and
 strong support,
A shelter from the heat, a shade from
 the noonday sun,
 a guard against stumbling, a help
 against falling.
²⁰He lifts up spirits, brings a sparkle
 to the eyes,
 gives health and life and blessing.

True Worship of God

²¹Ill-gotten goods offered in sacrifice
 are tainted.
²²Presents from the lawless do
 not win God's favor.
²³The Most High is not pleased with
 the gifts of the godless,
 nor for their many sacrifices
 does he forgive their sins.
²⁴One who slays a son in his father's
 presence—
 whoever offers sacrifice from
 the holdings of the poor.
²⁵The bread of charity is life itself
 for the needy;

In 34:14-20, the sage speaks of the benefits of reverencing the Lord, who supports his followers wherever they are. Indeed, trustful hope in God casts out fear (Ps 23:1-4; 1 John 4:18). The devout are fortunate, because God's eyes are on them to save them (Ps 33:18-19; 128:1). Even for the traveler, God is a shelter and a guard (Ps 121:5-6; Isa 25:4-5).

34:21–35:26 True worship of God

This long section on piety and social responsibility leads into a prayer for divine deliverance of the oppressed Israelites (36:1-22). Sirach 34:21-23 asserts that sacrifice is useless without a concern for justice (Isa 1:14-17; Amos 5:21-24). An offering from ill-gotten goods is unacceptable to God (Prov 21:27; Mal 1:6-8), and a multitude of sin-offerings does not bring forgiveness without repentance (Lev 4:13-21; Hos 8:13).

whoever withholds it is a murderer.

²⁶To take away a neighbor's living is to commit murder;

²⁷to deny a laborer wages is to shed blood.

²⁸If one builds up and another tears down,
what do they gain but trouble?

²⁹If one prays and another curses,
whose voice will God hear?

³⁰If one again touches a corpse after bathing,
what does he gain by the purification?

³¹So one who fasts for sins,
but goes and commits them again:
Who will hear his prayer,
what is gained by mortification?

35 ¹To keep the law is to make many offerings;

²whoever observes the commandments sacrifices a peace offering.

³By works of charity one offers fine flour,

⁴and one who gives alms presents a sacrifice of praise.

⁵To refrain from evil pleases the Lord,
and to avoid injustice is atonement.

⁶Do not appear before the Lord empty-handed,

⁷for all that you offer is in fulfillment of the precepts.

⁸The offering of the just enriches the altar:
a sweet odor before the Most High.

With prophetic vigor the sage condemns those who offer sacrifices from goods taken from the poor (34:24-27). Seizing a person's livelihood is as bad as slaying a son in his father's presence, the cruel punishment inflicted on Jerusalem's last king Zedekiah (2 Kgs 25:6-7). The God who is father of the poor (Ps 68:6; 103:13) cannot be pleased with sacrifices of goods stolen from the needy. Similarly, depriving laborers of their wages is equivalent to murder (Deut 24:14-15: Jas 5:4-6). In 1514, these verses helped Bartolomé de Las Casas to grasp the harmful effects of the Spanish conquest on the indigenous population of the Americas (*History of the Indies*, bk. 3, ch. 79).

Sirach 34:28-31 condemns insincerity in worship. A builder's labor is wasted if someone else destroys the building (Jer 45:4; Eccl 1:3). Likewise, if the oppressor offers prayers while his poor victims call out to God against him (Exod 22:22), God will hear the cry of the needy, rather than the oppressor's prayers (4:5-6). The law of Moses stipulated a ritual for being cleansed from the impurity contracted by touching a corpse (Num 19:11-12), but the purification rite is wasted if a person touches a dead body afterward (2 Pet 2:22). Likewise, those who fast for the forgiveness of their faults and then return to their sins obtain no benefit from their self-denial (Lev 16:29-30; Isa 58:3-7).

⁹The sacrifice of the just is accepted,
    never to be forgotten.
¹⁰With a generous spirit pay homage
    to the Lord,
    and do not spare your freewill
      gifts.
¹¹With each contribution show a
    cheerful countenance,
    and pay your tithes in a spirit of
      joy.
¹²Give to the Most High as he has
    given to you,
    generously, according to your
      means.
¹³For he is a God who always repays
    and will give back to you seven-
      fold.

¹⁴But offer no bribes; these he does
    not accept!
¹⁵Do not trust in sacrifice of the
    fruits of extortion,
For he is a God of justice,
    who shows no partiality.
¹⁶He shows no partiality to the weak
    but hears the grievance of the
      oppressed.

¹⁷He does not forsake the cry of the
    orphan,
    nor the widow when she pours
      out her complaint.
¹⁸Do not the tears that stream down
    her cheek
¹⁹cry out against the one that
    causes them to fall?
²⁰Those who serve God to please
    him are accepted;
    their petition reaches the clouds.
²¹The prayer of the lowly pierces the
    clouds;
    it does not rest till it reaches its
      goal;
Nor will it withdraw till the Most
    High responds,
²²judges justly and affirms the
    right.

God indeed will not delay,
    and like a warrior, will not be
      still
Till he breaks the backs of the
    merciless
²³and wreaks vengeance upon
    the nations;

According to 35:1-5, true worship involves upright deeds as well as religious devotion (Jas 1:27). The sage equates keeping the Torah with offering communion sacrifices (Lev 7:29-30; 1 Sam 15:22), while performing kindness is equivalent to presenting a grain offering to God (Lev 2:1-3; Mark 12:32-33). The sacrifice pleasing God is to turn away from evil and injustice (Job 1:1; 28:28).

Sirach 35:6-13 outlines the right attitude for worship. Rather than coming empty-handed (Exod 23:15; Deut 16:16), the person attending the temple liturgy should bring the prescribed offerings (7:29-31). The worship offered by the righteous is acceptable to God, because the sacrifice of their just deeds matches the offerings they make at the temple (Prov 21:3). In 35:10-11, freewill gifts were the priests' portion, while tithes were for the Levites' upkeep (Num 18:8-24; Tob 1:6-8). According to 35:12-13, worshipers can give joyfully because they trust that God will provide for them (Deut 14:22-29; 2 Cor 9:7-8). In response to God's abundant blessings, the sage urges

Till he destroys the scepter of the proud,
and cuts off the staff of the wicked;
²⁴Till he requites everyone according to their deeds,
and repays them according to their thoughts;
²⁵Till he defends the cause of his people,
and makes them glad by his salvation.
²⁶Welcome is his mercy in time of distress
as rain clouds in time of drought.

A Prayer for God's People

36 ¹Come to our aid, O God of the universe,
²and put all the nations in dread of you!
³Raise your hand against the foreign people,
that they may see your mighty deeds.
⁴As you have used us to show them your holiness,
so now use them to show us your glory.
⁵Thus they will know, as we know, that there is no God but you.

---

generosity "according to your means" (Lev 5:11; Tob 4:8). As Exodus 20:6 affirms, God rewards people for their good actions (12:2).

Sirach 35:14-22a asserts that the prayers of the needy will not go unheard. God cannot be bribed with sacrifices (Deut 10:17; Gal 6:7), especially offerings derived from inequitable dealings (Prov 15:8). Instead, God upholds justice (Gen 18:25; Deut 10:18) and shows no favoritism (2 Chr 19:7; Acts 10:34-35). Though not unduly partial toward the poor (Lev 19:15), God will certainly hear the cries of the victims of injustice (Prov 22:22-23), especially oppressed widows and orphans (Exod 22:21-22; Luke 18:1-8). Indeed, the pauper's cry pierces the clouds to reach God (Exod 3:9).

Using the image of the divine warrior (Exod 15:3; Isa 42:13), Sirach 35:22b-24 warns that oppressing the weak leads to judgment from the Almighty. Vengeance will come upon the "proud," presumably including the foreign rulers of Palestine in Ben Sira's lifetime (10:8), because God is able to repay people for their wicked deeds (Prov 24:12; Jer 25:14). In 35:25, Ben Sira is confident that God will plead Israel's cause (Isa 51:22) so that they can rejoice in his saving help (Isa 25:9). The Israelites yearn for God's merciful answer to their prayers, just as people long for rain clouds in a time of drought (Zech 10:1).

36:1-22 Prayer for divine deliverance

Although the strong nationalistic tone of this prayer has led some scholars to doubt that Ben Sira wrote it, various factors suggest that he is indeed its author. As in 24:10-11 and 50:1-21, Jerusalem is central in 36:18-19,

⁶Give new signs and work new
    wonders;
    ⁷show forth the splendor of your
        right hand and arm.
⁸Rouse your anger, pour out wrath;
    ⁹humble the enemy, scatter the
        foe.
¹⁰Hasten the ending, appoint the
    time,
    and let people proclaim your
        mighty deeds.
¹¹Let raging fire consume the fugi-
    tive,
    and your people's oppressors
        meet destruction.
¹²Crush the heads of the hostile
    rulers
    who say, "There is no one besides
        me."

¹³Gather all the tribes of Jacob,
    ¹⁶that they may inherit the land
        as in days of old.
¹⁷Show mercy to the people called
    by your name:
    Israel, whom you named your
        firstborn.
¹⁸Take pity on your holy city:
    Jerusalem, your dwelling place.
¹⁹Fill Zion with your majesty,
    your temple with your glory.

²⁰Give evidence of your deeds of
    old;
    fulfill the prophecies spoken in
        your name.
²¹Reward those who have hoped in
    you,
    and let your prophets be proved
        true.

---

and the sage's nationalistic feeling is also evident in 50:25-26. The plea for vengeance on the nations arises naturally out of his concern for the oppressed who call on the divine warrior for help (35:21-26). This prayer is in line with pleas for vengeance in the Hebrew Bible (Ps 94:1-7; Jer 10:25), though it differs from Jesus' call to forgive enemies (Matt 5:44). The absence of 36:14-15 does not reflect any missing text but is due to a dislocation in the Greek manuscripts.

The first stanza (36:1-5) prays for divine punishment of the pagan nations, presumably Israel's Hellenistic overlords—either the Ptolemies before 200 B.C. or the Seleucids thereafter. Pleading that the Gentiles be made to dread God, Ben Sira implicitly recalls the exodus and David's victories (Exod 15:16; 1 Chr 14:17). Whereas God has previously demonstrated justice by punishing the Israelites for their sins, now the prayer asks that God may show them mercy and thereby display holiness (Ezek 36:23). Thus the pagan nations will recognize that there is one true God (Ps 83:19; 1 Chr 17:20).

The second stanza (36:6-12) continues the appeal for divine punishment on Israel's foes. Ben Sira prays for God to renew his wonders, such as those performed through Moses at the time of the exodus (Exod 15:6; Ps 135:9). In 36:8, Ben Sira echoes earlier biblical prayers for God to pour out wrath on pagan nations (Jer 10:25; Ps 79:6). The sage asks God to humble the

²²Hear the prayer of your servants,
according to your good will
toward your people.
Thus all the ends of the earth will
know
that you are the eternal God.

Choice of Associates
²³The throat can swallow any food,
yet some foods are more agree-
able than others.
²⁴The palate tests delicacies put
forward as gifts,

---

enemy and defeat the foe, as David had done previously (47:5-7). Mention of the appointed time (36:10) recalls Habakkuk's promise of an occasion when foreign powers would no longer oppress Israel (Hab 2:3).

The third stanza (36:13-19) prays for the regathering of the scattered Israelites, in accordance with the hopes of the prophets (Jer 31:8; Ezek 39:27). Ben Sira begs that the dispersed Jews may inherit the promised land as the early Israelites did under Moses and Joshua (Deut 31:7; Josh 1:6), thereby restoring the situation as in days of old (Isa 51:9; Ps 44:2-4). Israel is called the Lord's people (Deut 28:10; Jer 14:9) and God's firstborn (Exod 4:22; Jer 31:9). Since Jerusalem is the holy city (Isa 52:1; Matt 27:53) and God's dwelling place (Exod 15:17), Ben Sira prays that the temple may be filled with divine glory (1 Kgs 8:11; Hag 2:7).

The final stanza (36:20-22) begs for the fulfillment of the biblical prophecies, so that the nations may recognize the true God (Ezek 36:36). Unlike earlier wisdom books of the Bible, Sirach has an interest in prophecy (48:1–49:10). The "deeds of old" (36:20) cover the divine election of Israel and the exodus (Isa 63:11-12; Ps 74:2). The hope offered by the prophets includes visions of God's rescue of the people from foreign nations (Ezek 34:13; Hab 2:3). As a result of the divine deliverance granted in answer to this prayer, Ben Sira asks that knowledge of the one true God will reach the ends of the earth (Isa 37:20; 45:22).

36:23–37:15 Discernment in relationships

This poem concerns discernment in making important relationships: with a wife (36:26-31), friends (37:1-6), and advisors (37:7-11). To illustrate the need for discernment, Ben Sira begins the poem by referring to the palate's selection of food (Job 12:11; 34:3).

Ben Sira then discusses the choice of wife from a male perspective. Sirach 36:26 indicates the low status of women, who were under the control of male authority figures. In second-century B.C. Jewish culture, men but not women were free to choose their spouse (Tob 7:10-13) because the marriage agreement was usually between the bridegroom and the bride's father. In

so does a keen mind test deceitful
tidbits.
²⁵One with a tortuous heart brings
about grief,
but an experienced person can
turn the tables on him.

²⁶A woman will accept any man as
husband,
but one woman will be preferable
to another.
²⁷A woman's beauty makes her
husband's face light up,
for it surpasses all else that delights the eye.
²⁸And if, besides, her speech is
soothing,
her husband's lot is beyond that
of mortal men.
²⁹A wife is her husband's richest
treasure,
a help like himself and a staunch
support.
³⁰A vineyard with no hedge will be
overrun;

and a man with no wife becomes
a homeless wanderer.
³¹Who will trust an armed band
that shifts from city to city?
Or a man who has no nest,
who lodges wherever night
overtakes him?

37 ¹Every friend declares friendship,
but there are friends who are
friends in name only.
²Is it not a sorrow unto death
when your other self becomes
your enemy?
³"Alas, my companion! Why were
you created
to fill the earth with deceit?"
⁴A harmful friend will look to your
table,
but in time of trouble he stands
aloof.
⁵A good friend will fight with you
against the foe,
and against your enemies he will
hold up your shield.

36:27 the sage acknowledges the effect that a woman's beauty has on her husband (26:16-18). If in addition she has kindly speech (Prov 15:4), her husband is very fortunate. Sirach 36:29 echoes Proverbs 18:22. As his help-mate and support (Gen 2:20; Tob 8:6), the wife also has a protective role toward her husband, like a vineyard fence defending it from wild beasts. Without a wife, a man can become a homeless wanderer (Gen 4:12). Sirach 36:31 recalls Proverbs 27:8.

In 37:1-6 the sage discusses the need to select friends carefully. Whereas anyone will claim to be loyal (Prov 20:6), some persons are not true friends. Betrayal by a supposed friend can produce a deathly sorrow, as Jesus found in Gethsemane (Matt 26:38). Despite sharing the same table (37:4), the fair-weather friend will be absent in one's time of need (6:10). By contrast, a good friend will come to one's defense against enemies, as David defended his fellow Israelites from the Philistine Goliath (1 Sam 17:32).

Sirach 37:7-11 advocates caution in choosing advisors, since some will offer advice simply out of self-interest. In line with his extreme wariness

⁶Do not forget your comrade during
the battle,
and do not neglect him when you
distribute your spoils.

⁷Every counselor points out a way,
but some counsel ways of their
own.
⁸Watch out when one offers advice;
find out first of all what he wants.
For he also may be thinking of
himself—
Why should the opportunity fall
to him?
⁹He may tell you how good your
way will be,
and then stand by to see you
impoverished.
¹⁰Seek no advice from your
father-in-law,
and from one who is envious of
you, keep your intentions
hidden.
¹¹Seek no advice from a woman
about her rival,
from a coward about war,
from a merchant about business,
from a buyer about value,
from a miser about generosity,
from a cruel person about wellbeing,
from a worthless worker about
his work,
from a seasonal laborer about
the harvest,
from an idle slave about a great
task—
pay no attention to any advice
they give.

¹²Instead, associate with a religious
person,
who you know keeps the commandments;
Who is like-minded with yourself
and will grieve for you if you
fall.
¹³Then, too, heed your own heart's
counsel;
for there is nothing you can
depend on more.
¹⁴The heart can reveal your situation
better than seven sentinels on a
tower.

(6:13; 8:18-19), the sage urges being on guard toward potential advisors until their motives become evident. Despite predicting a happy future, they may easily stand by and watch one's misfortune. Sirach 37:10-11 lists persons from whom it is unwise to seek advice. In 37:11, jealousy caused by polygamy is presupposed in the sage's advice not to consult with a woman about a rival wife (26:6). Wariness is needed with a buyer who is seeking to make a profit (Prov 20:14).

By contrast (37:12), it is wise to consult with a religious person who keeps the commandments (9:15), shares the same outlook, and is sympathetic. It is also important to listen to one's inner instincts, as a late Egyptian wisdom text declares: "One who listens to the judgment of his heart sleeps untroubled" (*Papyrus Insinger* 21.13). Indeed, a person's conscience is a more useful guide than seven astrologers observing the night sky from an observatory tower (Isa 47:13). Finally, the sage suggests seeking guidance from God, who can lead a person on the right path (Prov 3:6; Tob 4:19).

¹⁵Then with all this, pray to God
  to make your steps firm in the
    true path.

Wisdom and Temperance

¹⁶A word is the source of every deed;
  a thought, of every act.
¹⁷The root of all conduct is the heart;
  ¹⁸four branches it shoots forth:
Good and evil, death and life,
  and their absolute mistress is the
    tongue.
¹⁹One may be wise and benefit
  many,
  yet appear foolish to himself.
²⁰One may be wise, but if his words
  are rejected,
  he will be deprived of all enjoy-
    ment.

²²When one is wise to his own
  advantage,
  the fruits of knowledge are seen
    in his own person.
²³When one is wise to the advantage
  of people,
  the fruits of knowledge are
    lasting.
²⁴One wise for himself has full
  enjoyment,
  and all who see him praise him.
²⁵The days of one's life are
  numbered,
  but the life of Israel, days with-
    out number.
²⁶One wise among the people wins
  a heritage of glory,
  and his name lives on and on.

37:16-26 Wise speech

Sirach 37:16-18 emphasizes the primary role of language in human thought. As Genesis 1 describes God creating by means of the word, so for human beings every action begins with a thought expressed in language. Springing from the mind are four branches (or perhaps measuring sticks): good and evil, and death and life. The wording recalls the choice facing Israel in Deuteronomy 30:15: either life with prosperity (= good) if the people obeyed God, or else death together with doom (= evil) if they were disobedient. In this choice between life and death (Prov 18:21), the tongue has a crucial role (5:13).

Sirach 37:19-26 goes on to explore different kinds of wisdom (19:20-24). Despite seeming wise enough to teach others, individuals may fail to apply wisdom to their own lives, but those who apply good sense to themselves will benefit from it personally. Moreover, if someone deploys wisdom for the benefit of the whole people, the fruits of this knowledge will be enduring (24:33; 33:18). Israelites should use their understanding to help their people, because a person's lifespan is limited, whereas Israel's existence is everlasting (Jer 31:36). According to 37:24, the first to benefit from wisdom will be oneself, through receiving praise from everybody, while those who use wisdom to help the nation will inherit an eternal reputation (Prov 3:35).

²⁷My son, while you are well,
> govern your appetite,
> and see that you do not allow it
> > what is bad for you.
²⁸For not everything is good for
> everyone,
> nor is everything suited to every
> > taste.
²⁹Do not go to excess with any
> enjoyment,
> neither become a glutton for
> > choice foods;
³⁰For sickness comes with overeating,
> and gluttony brings on nausea.
³¹Through lack of self-control many
> have died,
> but the abstemious one prolongs
> > life.

Sickness and Death

38 ¹Make friends with the doctor,
> for he is essential to you;
> God has also established him in
> > his profession.
²From God the doctor has wisdom,
> and from the king he receives
> > sustenance.
³Knowledge makes the doctor dis-
> tinguished,
> and gives access to those in
> > authority.
⁴God makes the earth yield healing
> herbs
> which the prudent should not
> > neglect;
⁵Was not the water sweetened by a
> twig,

37:27–38:23 Health, medicine, sickness, and death

This section comprises four poems: on health (37:27-31), medicine (38:1-8), sickness (38:9-15), and death (38:16-23). Ben Sira begins with personal responsibility for one's health (preventive medicine), before speaking of the benefit of a physician. Sirach 37:27 encourages self-restraint in eating (31:19-20), because not every food benefits everyone (1 Cor 6:12; 10:23). Ben Sira specially addresses his young students, who would be invited to Greek-style banquets where food and drink were plentiful, and so he urges moderate enjoyment of the delicacies offered (Prov 25:16). His warning against overeating (37:30) may be illustrated by the unhappy experience of the grumbling Israelites, who became nauseous from excessive consumption of quail-meat (Num 11:18-20).

Sirach 38:1-8 contains a rare positive portrayal of medical doctors in the Bible (see also the description of Luke in Col 4:14). Because much ancient medicine was connected with pagan belief, King Asa's recourse to physicians (or healers) is viewed as indicating a lack of faith (2 Chr 16:12). However, Ben Sira sees no contradiction between utilizing God-given medicines (38:4) and praying for recovery (38:9). Perhaps the sage has in mind King Hezekiah, who in his sickness used a fig poultice (Isa 38:21) and also prayed earnestly to God (Isa 38:2-3).

so that all might learn his power?
⁶He endows people with knowledge,
to glory in his mighty works,
⁷Through which the doctor eases
pain,
⁸and the druggist prepares his
medicines.
Thus God's work continues without cease
in its efficacy on the surface of
the earth.

⁹My son, when you are ill, do not
delay,
but pray to God, for it is he who
heals.
¹⁰Flee wickedness and purify your
hands;
cleanse your heart of every sin.

¹¹Offer your sweet-smelling obla-
tion and memorial,
a generous offering according to
your means.
¹²Then give the doctor his place
lest he leave; you need him too,
¹³For there are times when recovery
is in his hands.
¹⁴He too prays to God
That his diagnosis may be correct
and his treatment bring about a
cure.
¹⁵Whoever is a sinner before his
Maker
will be defiant toward the
doctor.
¹⁶My son, shed tears for one who is
dead
with wailing and bitter lament;

Ben Sira regards the medical profession as divinely approved, since a physician's skill derives from God (38:1). Because medicinal herbs come from the Creator (Gen 1:12), they are not to be despised. Sirach 38:5 recalls Moses' action of purifying a foul-tasting water source at Marah by throwing a branch into it (Exod 15:23-25). Ben Sira sees this biblical incident as divine authorization for using medicinal plants. The gift of knowledge enables humanity to benefit from God's great works (42:21-23).

Having praised the physician in 38:1-8, Ben Sira now urges his students to seek healing when required, through prayer (Jas 5:14-16) and through medical assistance (38:9-15). The first step to health is purifying one's heart by turning away from evil and by offering sacrifice for sin (Lev 5:11-13)—though other biblical texts indicate that by no means all sickness is due to sin (Job 2:7-10; John 9:2). After praying, the sick person is advised to seek help from the physician (38:12). Trusting in God and seeking medical help are not incompatible, since God's healing frequently comes through medical means. Indeed, the devout physician also prays to God for success in diagnosing and treating the patient.

After recommending his students to make use of medical help in times of sickness (38:9-15), Ben Sira discusses how to behave when death has

As is only proper, prepare the body,
and do not absent yourself from
the burial.
¹⁷Weeping bitterly, mourning fully,
pay your tribute of sorrow, as
deserved:
A day or two, to prevent gossip;
then compose yourself after
your grief.
¹⁸For grief can bring on death,
and heartache can sap one's
strength.
¹⁹When a person is carried away,
sorrow is over;
and the life of the poor one is
grievous to the heart.

²⁰Do not turn your thoughts to him
again;
cease to recall him; think rather
of the end.
²¹Do not recall him, for there is no
hope of his return;
you do him no good, and you
harm yourself.
²²Remember that his fate will also
be yours;
for him it was yesterday, for you
today.
²³With the dead at rest, let memory
cease;
be consoled, once the spirit has
gone.

occurred (38:16-23). He advises moderation in mourning rather than hoping in a future life (17:27-28; 41:3-4), because no clear doctrine of the afterlife had developed before his lifetime (Job 14:7-12; Ps 115:17). For Christians, Ben Sira's teaching is completed with the later doctrine of the resurrection (1 Cor 15).

Sirach 38:16 recognizes the rightness of weeping for the dead (22:11) and carrying out a proper funeral (Tob 4:3-4; 14:12-13). It is a mistake to be absent from the burial rites, whether from disregard of the deceased or an unwillingness to make any contribution. The sage advises a couple of days of mourning, presumably for a deceased friend. For family members and important persons (Gen 50:10; Jdt 16:24), the Bible mentions a seven-day period of mourning (22:12). Aware that excessive mourning can bring on depression (Prov 15:13; 2 Cor 7:10), the sage advises a limit to grieving (30:21).

Sirach 38:20-23 cautions against brooding after a bereavement. The deceased person has no hope of returning to earthly life, and the sage offers no expectation of an afterlife (contrast Dan 12:2-3; 1 Thess 4:13-14). Hence, constant thought of the departed person will only cause depression (Gen 44:27-29; 2 Sam 12:23). Ben Sira instead counsels a firm awareness of one's own mortality (7:36; 8:7). Once the deceased has been laid to rest, his or her memory should also be allowed to rest.

Vocations of the Skilled Worker and the Scribe

²⁴The scribe's wisdom increases wisdom;
  whoever is free from toil can become wise.
²⁵How can one become learned who guides the plow,
  and thrills in wielding the goad like a lance,
Who guides the ox and urges on the bullock,
  and whose every concern is for cattle?
²⁶His concern is to plow furrows,
  and he is careful to fatten the livestock.

²⁷So with every engraver and designer
  who, laboring night and day,
Fashions carved seals,
  and whose concern is to vary the pattern.

His determination is to produce a lifelike impression,
  and he is careful to finish the work.

²⁸So too the smith sitting by the anvil, intent on the iron he forges.
The flame from the fire sears his flesh,
  yet he toils away in the furnace heat.
The clang of the hammer deafens his ears;
  his eyes are on the object he is shaping.
His determination is to finish the work,
  and he is careful to perfect it in detail.

²⁹So also the potter sitting at his labor,
  revolving the wheel with his feet.
He is always concerned for his products,

DEMONSTRATING THE RESULTS OF WISDOM

Sirach 38:24–42:14

38:24–39:11 Vocations of manual workers and scribes

In order to encourage his students to acquire wisdom through study, Ben Sira praises the scribal profession in comparison with various skilled manual trades (farmer, seal engraver, smith, potter). The incentive for the student is the scribe's honorable status (39:4) and reputation (39:9-11), in contrast with the artisan's hard work (38:25-30) and less honorable position in society (38:32-33).

Ben Sira draws on an ancient Egyptian writing known as the *Satire of the Trades*, which promises wealth for the successful student. Whereas the Egyptian text compares manual laborers unfavorably to the scribe, Ben Sira recognizes the need for such workers in any community (38:31-32), because physical labor was divinely decreed (7:15). Despite the value and necessity of manual work, Ben Sira begins by asserting the scribe's need for leisure to acquire wisdom (38:24).

and turns them out in quantity.
³⁰With his hands he molds the clay,
and with his feet softens it.
His determination is to complete
the glazing,
and he is careful to fire the kiln.
³¹All these are skilled with their
hands,
each one an expert at his own
work;
³²Without them no city could be
lived in,
and wherever they stay, they do
not go hungry.
But they are not sought out for the
council of the people,
³³nor are they prominent in the
assembly.
They do not sit on the judge's bench,
nor can they understand law and
justice.
They cannot expound discipline or
judgment,

nor are they found among the
rulers.
³⁴Yet they maintain the fabric of the
world,
and their concern is for exercise
of their skill.

39 How different the person who
devotes himself
to the study of the law of the
Most High!
¹He explores the wisdom of all the
ancients
and is occupied with the
prophecies;
²He preserves the discourses of the
famous,
and goes to the heart of involved
sayings;
³He seeks out the hidden meaning
of proverbs,
and is busied with the enigmas
found in parables.

In 38:25-30 Ben Sira shows the hardships of four of the eighteen trades listed in the Egyptian text: farmer (1 Kgs 19:19), seal maker (Exod 28:11), smith (Neh 3:32), and potter (Jer 18:2-6). After sampling the work of artisans involved in these four trades, Ben Sira acknowledges that these workers have their own valuable skills (38:31-33). He admits that all these occupations are necessary for the wellbeing of society, much as St. Paul speaks of a variety of roles being needed within the church community (1 Cor 12:27-30). However, 38:33 notes that artisans rarely become prominent in government.

After considering various trades, Ben Sira speaks favorably of the scribal profession (39:1-11). This description is often taken as a self-portrait. The scribe is depicted as giving his whole attention to the revealed word of God (Ps 1:2). In 39:1-2 Ben Sira mentions the "law of the Most High," the "prophecies," and the "discourses of the famous." These categories largely reflect the contents of the Hebrew Scriptures, later divided into three sections (law, prophets, and writings). As noted in 8:8, the learned scribe will gain an honored position in the service of princes (39:4), presumably at court (Prov 22:29). While serving on government missions abroad, the

⁴He is in attendance on the great,
and appears before rulers.
He travels among the peoples of
foreign lands
to test what is good and evil
among people.
⁵His care is to rise early
to seek the Lord his Maker,
to petition the Most High,
To open his mouth in prayer,
to ask pardon for his sins.

⁶If it pleases the Lord Almighty,
he will be filled with the spirit of
understanding;
He will pour forth his words of
wisdom
and in prayer give praise to the
Lord.
⁷He will direct his knowledge and
his counsel,
as he meditates upon God's
mysteries.
⁸He will show the wisdom of what
he has learned
and glory in the Law of the
Lord's covenant.

⁹Many will praise his understanding;
his name can never be blotted
out;
Unfading will be his memory,
through all generations his name
will live;
¹⁰Peoples will speak of his wisdom,
and the assembly will declare
his praise.
¹¹While he lives he is one out of a
thousand,
and when he dies he leaves a
good name.

Praise of God the Creator

¹²Once more I will set forth my theme
to shine like the moon in its fullness!
¹³Listen to me, my faithful children:
open up your petals,
like roses planted near running
waters;
¹⁴Send up the sweet odor of incense,
break forth in blossoms like the
lily.

---

scribe's mind will be broadened, just as Ben Sira himself has gained wisdom through his travels (34:9-13).

Whereas other workers give close attention to their tasks, the scribe's first thought is to seek God in prayer (39:5), aware of the daily need for divine forgiveness (8:5; 17:25). Then the Lord will grant a spirit of wisdom (Isa 11:2; Eph 1:17) and stir up the praise of God (39:15). Through the scribe's teaching, others will benefit from his wisdom (33:18; 51:25-28). Sirach 39:9-11 describes the honorable status achieved by the scribe (37:22-26; 44:13-15).

39:12-35 God as source of everything good

A difficult question for religious believers is the problem of God's justice in the face of evil (theodicy). If God is good, how is it that innocent people suffer? If God created a good world (Gen 1:31), why does evil exist? While some biblical passages suggest that God is the source of everything, evil as well as good (Job 2:10; Isa 45:7), other texts attribute the origin of evil to

Raise your voices in a chorus of
praise;
bless the Lord for all his works!
¹⁵Proclaim the greatness of his name,
loudly sing his praises,
With music on the harp and all
stringed instruments;
sing out with joy as you proclaim:

¹⁶The works of God are all of them
good;
he supplies for every need in its
own time.
¹⁷At his word the waters become
still as in a flask;
he had but to speak and the
reservoirs were made.
¹⁸He has but to command and his
will is done;
nothing can limit his saving
action.

¹⁹The works of all humankind are
present to him;
nothing is hidden from his eyes.
²⁰His gaze spans all the ages:
is there any limit to his saving
action?
To him, nothing is small or insignificant,
and nothing too wonderful or
hard for him.
²¹No cause then to say: "What is the
purpose of this?"
Everything is chosen to satisfy a
need.

²²His blessing overflows like the Nile;
like the Euphrates it enriches the
surface of the earth.
²³Even so, his wrath dispossesses
the nations
and turns fertile land into a salt
marsh.

---

human sin (Gen 3:17; Rom 5:12) or to the activity of Satan (Wis 2:24; Job 2:7). Since Ben Sira has no doubt about God's goodness, he places his treatment of the question of theodicy within a hymn of praise to God the Creator.

Just as the psalms frequently praise the Lord for being good (Pss 118:1; 136:1), so 39:16 praises God for good deeds (Ps 111:7) and for supplying every need in its own time (Eccl 3:1-8). In the Creator's providence (Ps 33:7), water can serve a good or a bad purpose. God used water to deliver the Israelites from slavery at the exodus but to punish their oppressors (Exod 15:8-10; Wis 11:6-14). In asserting that God has made everything suitable for its purpose (39:21), Ben Sira matches the Stoic view that everything in the universe has its own useful function. Thus, the philosopher Chrysippus (d. ca. 206 B.C.) taught that mice served the purpose of encouraging human beings to be tidy (Plutarch, *On Stoic Self-Contradictions*, 1044D).

Sirach 39:22-24 asserts that both blessing and curse from God serve the divine plan (11:14). The expulsion of the nations (39:23) refers to Joshua's conquest of the promised land (Josh 11:16-23), blamed on the sinfulness of the territory's former inhabitants (Gen 15:16; 1 Kgs 21:26). Just as God's blessing causes dry farmland to be irrigated by seasonal flooding, so God's curse turns fertile soil into a salty waste as a punishment for people's disobedience (Ps 107:33-34).

²⁴For the virtuous his paths are level,
    to the haughty they are clogged
        with stones.
²⁵Good things for the good he pro-
        vided from the beginning,
    but for the wicked good things
        and bad.
²⁶Chief of all needs for human life
    are water and fire, iron and salt,
The heart of the wheat, milk and
        honey,
    the blood of the grape, and oil,
        and clothing.
²⁷For the good all these are good,
    but for the wicked they turn out
        evil.

²⁸There are stormwinds created to
        punish;
    in their fury they can dislodge
        mountains.
In a time of destruction they hurl
        their force

and calm the anger of their
        Maker.
²⁹Fire and hail, famine and disease:
    these too were created for
        punishment.
³⁰Ravenous beasts, scorpions, vipers,
    and the avenging sword to
        exterminate the wicked:
All these were created to meet a
        need,
    and are kept in his storehouse for
        the proper time.
³¹When he commands them, they
        rejoice,
    in their assigned tasks they do not
        disobey his command.

³²That is why from the first I took my
        stand,
    and wrote down as my theme:
³³The works of God are all of them
        good;
    he supplies for every need in its
        own time.

Right from the beginning God has made good things for good people (39:25). By contrast, the wicked receive not just good things, but bad things as well (40:8-10). Sirach 39:26 lists ten essentials for human life (29:21). Besides drinking water, a person needs fire for heating food, iron for pans, and salt for cooking. Mention of milk and honey together recalls God's promise of the holy land to the Israelites (Exod 3:8), while the "blood of the grape" is a poetic phrase meaning wine (Gen 49:11; Deut 32:14). Clothing is mentioned as a necessity in Genesis 28:20, along with bread.

While God has created all things good, they help the virtuous but ulti-mately harm the wicked (39:27). There is certainly some truth in this view; for instance, money can serve many useful purposes for someone who knows how to benefit from it, but it can ruin a greedy person (31:5-8). Simi-larly, wine can bring joy to sensible people but may harm the foolish (31:27-30). Nevertheless, this explanation does not solve all the problems of theodicy.

As a divine punishment (39:28), the winds that normally bring fresh air can become hurricanes. Besides storm winds, Ben Sira lists eight things

³⁴There is no cause then to say:
"This is not as good as that";
for each shows its worth at the
proper time.
³⁵So now with full heart and voice
proclaim
and bless his name!

Joys and Miseries of Life

40 ¹A great anxiety has God
allotted,
and a heavy yoke, to the children
of Adam,
From the day they leave their
mother's womb
until the day they return to the
mother of all the living.
²Troubled thoughts and fear of
heart are theirs

and anxious foreboding until
death.
³Whether one sits on a lofty throne
or grovels in dust and ashes,
⁴Whether one wears a splendid
crown
or is clothed in the coarsest of
garments—
⁵There is wrath and envy, trouble
and dread,
terror of death, fury and strife.
Even when one lies on his bed to
rest,
his cares disturb his sleep at
night.
⁶So short is his rest it seems like
none,
till in his dreams he struggles as
he did by day,

(39:29-30) which God uses to punish evildoers (Lev 26:14-22; Deut 28:20-24). In the form of lightning, fire can destroy the wicked (2 Kgs 1:10; Luke 9:54). Famine and pestilence were regarded as divine punishments on Israel for failing to keep the Torah (1 Kgs 8:37; Jer 21:9), as also were attacks from wild beasts and snakes (Deut 32:24; 2 Kgs 17:25). Ben Sira regards everything as available for God's use in blessing or punishing (Ps 148:8). So in 39:33 the sage restates his original assertion (39:16): God fulfills every need in its proper time (Eccl 3:1). Hence God deserves to be praised for the providential ordering of the universe (Ps 96:2; 103:1).

40:1-17 Life's burdens

The human life that begins in one's mother's womb (Job 1:21; Ps 139:13) ends with a return to the "mother of all the living"—not a reference to Eve (Gen 3:20) but to mother earth (Gen 3:19). Anxieties affect kings on their thrones (Eccl 1:12-14) as much as poor people sitting on the ground (31:1-4). Sirach 40:5 lists seven causes of anxiety that can even disturb a person's sleep (Eccl 2:23; Job 7:3-4).

After listing these psychological woes, Ben Sira describes external troubles that afflict all human beings, but especially the wicked (40:8-10). The sage asserts that calamities such as war and disease affect the wicked seven times as much as they affect the virtuous (39:28-30). Ben Sira echoes

Troubled by the visions of his mind,
like a fugitive fleeing from the
pursuer.
⁷As he reaches safety, he wakes up,
astonished that there was nothing to fear.
⁸To all flesh, human being and
beast,
but for sinners seven times more,
⁹Come plague and bloodshed, fiery
heat and drought,
plunder and ruin, famine and
death.
¹⁰For the wicked evil was created,
and because of them destruction
hastens.

¹¹All that is of earth returns to earth,
and what is from above returns
above.
¹²All that comes from bribes or
injustice will be wiped out,
but loyalty remains forever.

¹³Wealth from injustice is like a
flooding wadi,
like a mighty stream with lightning and thunder,
¹⁴Which, in its rising, rolls along the
stones,
but suddenly, once and for all,
comes to an end.
¹⁵The offshoot of violence will not
flourish,
for the root of the godless is on
sheer rock.
¹⁶They are like reeds on riverbanks,
withered before all other plants;
¹⁷But goodness, like eternity, will
never be cut off,
and righteousness endures forever.

¹⁸Wealth or wages can make life
sweet,
but better than either, finding a
treasure.

---

the Torah that lists such punishments for disobeying God's covenant (Deut 28:15-68).

Sirach 40:11-17 depicts the bad effects of evildoing. Human physical life, originally created from the earth (Gen 2:7; 3:19), will go back to the earth (Eccl 3:20; Job 34:15), while the spirit will return to God at death (Eccl 12:7). Far from escaping mortality (Pss 49:14-21; 146:3-4), the impious will die like other mortals, but the deeds of the virtuous will be remembered forever (41:10-11). Wealth gained from injustice (40:13-14) is compared to a desert stream in full spate that quickly dries up (Job 6:15-17). The brief prosperity of the godless is as short-lived as the flourishing of reeds at the riverside (Job 8:11-12; Wis 4:3-5), whereas justice lasts forever (Prov 10:25; Wis 1:15).

40:18-27 A decalogue of good things

Here Ben Sira lists ten of life's good things, culminating in the fear of the Lord. Although profit gained from business and the wages gained from one's labor can sweeten life (Eccl 2:10; 3:12-13), it is better to find a treasure, perhaps a symbol of the gift of wisdom (20:30-31) or a good wife (36:29).

¹⁹A child or a city will preserve one's name,
   but better than either, finding wisdom.
Cattle and orchards make a person flourish;
   but better than either, a devoted wife.
²⁰Wine and strong drink delight the soul,
   but better than either, love of friends.
²¹Flute and harp offer sweet melody,
   but better than either, a pure tongue.
²²Grace and beauty delight the eye,
   but better than either, the produce of the field.
²³A friend and a neighbor are timely guides,

but better than either, a sensible wife.
²⁴Relatives and helpers for times of stress;
   but better than either, charity that rescues.
²⁵Gold and silver make one's way secure,
   but better than either, sound judgment.
²⁶Wealth and vigor make the heart exult,
   but better than either, fear of God.
In the fear of the Lord there is no want;
   whoever has it need seek no other support.
²⁷The fear of God is a paradise of blessings;

According to 40:19, a person's name can be preserved through offspring (Deut 25:5-6) or through establishing a city (Gen 4:17; 2 Sam 5:9), but a better way to preserve one's good name is by living wisely (44:14-15). Whereas a successful farm produces the nourishment for a healthy life, a better contribution to a man's health comes from a devoted wife (26:13). According to 40:20, more delightful than liquor is "love of friends" (Syriac translation), though the Hebrew text refers to conjugal love (Song 1:2).

A true voice is a more pleasant sound than music (40:21). While human beauty delights the eye, more beautiful are the wild flowers (Matt 6:28-30). Whereas friends may offer temporary advice (37:7), better guidance comes from a prudent wife (Prov 19:14; 31:26). According to 40:24, while brothers and sisters help at a time of trouble (Prov 17:17), charitable giving provides a better protection against distress (Prov 11:4; Tob 12:9).

In spite of denials in Psalm 49:17-21 and Luke 12:15, Sirach 40:25 asserts that money makes a person secure. However, more useful than money are sound judgment and good advice, as the story of King Rehoboam shows (1 Kgs 12:13-15). While economic and physical strength are important, greater security is provided by fear of God (1:11-13; 25:10-11), as earlier biblical teaching notes (Prov 14:26-27; 22:4). Indeed, fear of God is like the garden of Eden before Adam's sin (Gen 2:8-17; Isa 51:3).

its canopy is over all that is
glorious.
²⁸My son, do not live the life of a
beggar;
better to die than to beg.
²⁹When one has to look to a
stranger's table,
life is not worth living.
The delicacies offered bring revul-
sion of spirit,
and to the intelligent, inward
torture.
³⁰In the mouth of the shameless
begging is sweet,
but within him it burns like fire.

41 ¹O death! How bitter is the
thought of you
for the one at peace in his home,
For the one who is serene and always
successful,
who can still enjoy life's
pleasures.
²O death! How welcome is your
sentence

to the weak, failing in strength,
Stumbling and tripping on everything,
with sight gone and hope lost.
³Do not fear death's decree for you;
remember, it embraces those
before you and those to
come.
⁴This decree for all flesh is from God;
why then should you reject a law
of the Most High?
Whether one has lived a thousand
years, a hundred, or ten,
in Sheol there are no arguments
about life.

⁵The children of sinners are a repro-
bate line,
and witless offspring are in the
homes of the wicked.
⁶The inheritance of children of
sinners will perish,
and on their offspring will be
perpetual disgrace.

40:28–41:15 Life and death

This section concerns the opposite of life, as seen from various view-points: begging, which is a life not worth living (40:28-30); death, welcome or unwelcome (41:1-4); and the empty life of the godless (41:5-13). Sirach 40:28 asserts that it is better to die than to beg (29:22-23), because of the associated shame (Luke 16:3). Shameless people find sweetness in food given freely, because they do not have to pay for it, but in the end it will be as destructive as fire (Prov 6:27; Job 20:12-15).

Sirach 41:1-2 notes that death may be welcome to a sufferer but unwelcome to a healthy person (Job 3:21; 21:23-26). Paradoxically (Eccl 3:2), the evil of death can appear good to someone with very poor health (30:17). Ben Sira advises acceptance of death in its time, not because of a hope in the resurrection, but rather because it is the divine decree (14:17; 17:1-2), as Genesis shows (Gen 2:17; 3:19). While death is the universal fate of humanity (14:18; 38:22), Sirach 41:4 suggests that the sage has no hope of an afterlife (Eccl 6:3-6; 9:10), unlike some texts written after the Maccabean revolt (Dan 12:1-3; 2 Macc 7:9; 12:44-45).

⁷Children curse their wicked father,
  for they suffer disgrace because
    of him.
⁸Woe to you, O wicked people,
  who forsake the Law of the
    Most High.
⁹If you have children, calamity will
    be theirs;
  and if you beget them, it will be
    only for groaning.
When you stumble, there is lasting
    joy;
  and when you die, you become
    a curse.
¹⁰All that is nought returns to nought,
  so too the godless—from void to
    void.

¹¹The human body is a fleeting thing,
  but a virtuous name will never
    be annihilated.
¹²Have respect for your name, for it
  will stand by you

more than thousands of precious
    treasures.
¹³The good things of life last a
    number of days,
  but a good name, for days with-
    out number.

True and False Shame

¹⁴ᵇHidden wisdom and concealed
    treasure,
  of what value is either?
¹⁵Better is the person who hides his
    folly
  than the one who hides his
    wisdom.
¹⁴ᵃMy children, listen to instruction
    about shame;
¹⁶ᵃjudge of disgrace according to
    my rules,
¹⁶ᵇNot every kind of shame is
    shameful,
  nor is every kind of disgrace to
    be recognized.

Ben Sira now reflects on the unhappy earthly fate of the wicked (41:5-10), whose descendants are unsuccessful and whose name is a disgrace (Job 18:17-21; Ps 21:11). According to the sage, sinners' children lose their power and gain dishonor (Wis 3:17-19; 4:19). Against the usual biblical pattern for family life (Deut 27:16; Prov 31:28), these children will curse a father whose wickedness has caused them disgrace (Wis 12:10-11). Sirach 41:8 laments those who forsake the Torah (49:4), a great temptation to Ben Sira's students because of the strong influence of pagan Greek culture around that time (2 Macc 4:12-17). Whereas the human body decays (41:11), a good reputation is permanent, more precious than treasures (Prov 10:7; 22:1).

41:16–42:8 Appropriate and inappropriate shame

In Ben Sira's culture, shame was a strong motivating force to keep social and moral order, but he did not think people were always ashamed of the right things (4:21), so he lists things that deserve shame (moral lapses and breaches of social etiquette), as well as other items that do not require shame.

¹⁷Before father and mother be
   ashamed of immorality,
 before prince and ruler, of falsehood;
¹⁸Before master and mistress, of
   deceit;
 before the public assembly, of
   crime;
Before associate and friend, of dis-
   loyalty,
   ¹⁹and in the place where you
     settle, of theft.
Be ashamed of breaking an oath or
   a covenant,
 and of stretching your elbow at
   dinner;
Of refusing to give when asked,
   ²¹of rebuffing your own relatives;
Of defrauding another of his
   appointed share,
   ²⁰ᵃof failing to return a greeting;
²¹ᶜOf gazing at a man's wife,
   ²⁰ᵇof entertaining thoughts about
     another woman;
²²Of trifling with a servant girl you
   have,
 of violating her bed;

Of using harsh words with friends,
 of following up your gifts with
   insults;
42 ¹Of repeating what you hear,
   of betraying any secret.
Be ashamed of the right things,
 and you will find favor in the
   sight of all.

But of these things do not be
   ashamed,
 lest you sin to save face:
²Of the Law of the Most High and
   his precepts,
 or of justice that acquits the ungodly;
³Of sharing the expenses of a business or a journey,
 of dividing an inheritance or
   property;
⁴Of accuracy of scales and balances,
 of tested measures and weights;
Of acquiring much or little,
   ⁵of bargaining in dealing with a
     merchant;
Of constant training of children,

Sirach 41:17–42:1 provides a list of twenty disgraceful things. The first seven items all involve a breach of trust in word or deed, while the next five things concern thoughtless or unkind behavior. The following four disgraceful items are sexual misdeeds, starting with looks (Matt 5:28) and ending with deeds (9:8-9), and the last four examples concern breaches of friendship (18:15; 22:22).

After listing actions to be ashamed of, Ben Sira catalogs things for which one need not apologize (42:2-8). The first item is the Torah (42:2). Soon after Ben Sira's day, many Jewish males became ashamed of the Mosaic law and tried to disguise their circumcision (1 Macc 1:15). The second example means perhaps: "Do not be so ashamed of passing judgment that you let someone guilty go unpunished" (cf. Prov 24:23-24). The following six items concern proper business practices: fair division of costs and benefits, honest weights and measures (Prov 11:1; 16:11), and robust commercial dealings (37:11).

of beating the sides of a wicked
servant;
⁶Of a seal to keep a foolish wife at
home,
of a key where there are many
hands;
⁷Of numbering every deposit,
of recording all that is taken in
and given out;
⁸Of chastisement for the silly and
the foolish,
for the aged and infirm answer-
ing for wanton conduct.

Thus you will be truly refined
and recognized by all as discreet.

A Father's Care for His Daughter

⁹A daughter is a treasure that keeps
her father wakeful,
and worry over her drives away
sleep:
Lest in her youth she remain unmarried,
or when she is married, lest she
be childless;

The next four items that do not warrant shame concern managing a household (42:5-6), as viewed from a patriarchal standpoint (30:1-13; 33:25-33). Modern appreciation of human dignity means that we find it abhorrent that slaves were beaten and wives "sealed" by keeping them indoors. Mention of a "key" where there are many hands may refer to securing household goods against theft, or could refer to keeping an unmarried girl at home, away from the unwanted attentions of young men. The next two items involve the scribal task of keeping records, while the final pair of items concerns use of wisdom to chastise the foolish and undisciplined (Prov 19:25; Dan 13:52-59).

42:9-14 Paternal concern for daughters

The previous poem on shame leads Ben Sira to consider the care of daughters, since female relatives can bring great honor or dishonor to a male within a patriarchal shame culture. By modern standards, Ben Sira's writing is objectionable. In Hellenistic Judaism, as in Greek society of that time, there was a tendency to confine girls and even women to the home (2 Macc 3:19). Thus, Philo in the first century A.D. wrote: "Women are best suited to the indoor life which never strays from the house" (*Special Laws* 3.169).

Like a man who is sleepless when guarding something precious at home (42:9), a Jewish father in Ben Sira's time keeps anxious watch over a daughter (7:24-25). The patriarchal concern is for her to marry, to remain pure, and to be fertile. The father's worry about her when she is unmarried

¹⁰While unmarried, lest she be
defiled,
or in her husband's house, lest
she prove unfaithful;
Lest she become pregnant in her
father's house,
or be sterile in that of her husband.
¹¹My son, keep a close watch on
your daughter,
lest she make you a laughingstock for your enemies,
A byword in the city and the
assembly of the people,
an object of derision in public
gatherings.
See that there is no lattice in her
room,
or spot that overlooks the approaches to the house.
¹²Do not let her reveal her beauty to
any male,
or spend her time with married
women;
¹³For just as moths come from garments,
so a woman's wickedness comes
from a woman.

---

involves three scenarios (42:9-10): that she does not find a husband, or is defiled by rape or seduction (in which case it would be hard to find a bridegroom for her), or becomes pregnant while still under her father's care.

But when she is married, her father is still concerned that his daughter may disgrace him (42:9-10), though he need not worry about her anymore (7:25). Now the concern involves three other scenarios: that she will be hated by her husband (here the New American Bible has "sterile"), or be unfaithful to him, or prove unable to bear him a child (Gen 30:23; Luke 1:25).

The sage urges paternal vigilance over an unmarried daughter, so as to avoid any family shame (42:11). Indeed, Ben Sira even advises forbidding a lattice in her room, in case a man might see her beauty (Prov 7:6; Song 2:9). Similarly, an Alexandrian Jew of the first century B.C. or A.D. taught: "Guard a virgin in firmly locked rooms, and let her not be seen outside the house until her wedding day" (*Pseudo-Phocylides* 215–16).

Sirach 42:12 also prohibits an unmarried daughter from spending time with married women, presumably because they would talk frankly about their experience of marriage. The sage's chauvinistic view in 42:13 seems to be that corruption is hidden in women like a moth lurking in a garment (Job 13:28; Isa 50:9). While the Masada Hebrew text of 42:14b appears to say: "Better a reverent [or: fearful] daughter than any disgrace," another reading of the manuscript is: "Better a reverent daughter than a shameless son."

¹⁴Better a man's harshness than a
woman's indulgence,
a frightened daughter than any
disgrace.

The Works of God in Nature

¹⁵Now will I recall God's works;
what I have seen, I will describe.
By the LORD's word his works were
brought into being;
he accepts the one who does his
will.
¹⁶As the shining sun is clear to all,
so the glory of the LORD fills all
his works;
¹⁷Yet even God's holy ones must fail
in recounting the wonders of the
LORD,
Though God has given his hosts the
strength
to stand firm before his glory.
¹⁸He searches out the abyss and
penetrates the heart;
their secrets he understands.
For the Most High possesses all
knowledge,
and sees from of old the things
that are to come.
¹⁹He makes known the past and the
future,
and reveals the deepest secrets.
²⁰He lacks no understanding;

WISDOM IN CREATION AND HISTORY

Sirach 42:15–50:24

42:15–43:33 Praise of God's works in creation

As a preparation for the Praise of the Ancestors (44:1–50:24), Ben Sira celebrates God's marvelous creation. According to 42:15, the purpose of the hymn is to recall God's actions (Ps 77:12) and recount what the sage has seen (Job 15:17). God created the universe through the word (Gen 1:3; John 1:3), and the divine glory shines as clearly as sunlight (Ps 19:2-7; Rom 1:20). Despite being in God's presence, angels ("holy ones") are not fully aware of the marvels of divine power (Job 15:15).

The omniscient God searches inscrutable regions (42:18), not only the depths of the sea (Job 38:16), but also the human heart (Prov 15:11; Jdt 8:14). According to 42:18-22, God's knowledge includes the past and the future (Isa 41:21-23), since God sees all the ages (39:20) while remaining unchanging. Hence there is no addition or subtraction with God (Eccl 3:14), nor is there any need for an advisor (Isa 40:13; Rom 11:34).

Ben Sira next acknowledges the beautiful harmony of creation (42:23-25), in which everything created has a stable form of existence. Ben Sira does not mean that every creature lives forever, since both humans and animals die (14:17-18; 41:3). Rather, each creature exists for a particular purpose. In fact, God has created the world with a balance of opposites (11:14; 33:14-15), such as light and darkness (Gen 1:3-5; Isa 45:7).

no single thing escapes him.
²¹He regulates the mighty deeds of
his wisdom;
he is from all eternity one and
the same,
With nothing added, nothing taken
away;
no need of a counselor for him!
²²How beautiful are all his works,
delightful to gaze upon and a
joy to behold!
²³Everything lives and abides forever;
and to meet each need all things
are preserved.
²⁴All of them differ, one from
another,
yet none of them has he made in
vain;
²⁵For each in turn, as it comes, is
good;
can one ever see enough of their
splendor?

43 ¹The beauty of the celestial
height and the pure firmament,
heaven itself manifests its glory.
²The sun at its rising shines at its
fullest,
a wonderful instrument, the
work of the Most High!
³At noon it scorches the earth,
and who can bear its fiery heat?
⁴Like a blazing furnace of solid metal,
the sun's rays set the mountains
aflame;
Its fiery tongue consumes the world;
the eyes are burned by its fire.
⁵Great indeed is the LORD who
made it,
at whose orders it urges on its
steeds.
⁶It is the moon that marks the
changing seasons,
governing the times, their lasting
sign.

Next Ben Sira enumerates God's works, visible in the sky and the weather (43:1-22). Whereas Jewish apocalyptic writers and Greek scientists tried in various ways to explain the phenomena of the skies, Ben Sira contented himself with observing creation and praising God for it.

According to 43:2, the sun is not a god as in pagan religion (Egyptian Ra or Greek Apollo), but is rather the work of the Most High. Like a white-hot furnace, the noonday sun scorches the land (Ps 104:32). Sirach 43:5 recalls the ancient picture of the sun as drawn across the sky by horses (2 Kgs 23:11). According to 43:6-7, the moon marks the changing seasons of the Israelite religious calendar (Exod 12:2; Ps 104:19). The beauty of the rainbow (43:11) is a reason for praising its Maker (Gen 9:13; Ezek 1:28).

Sirach 43:13 regards the storm as manifesting God's power (Pss 18:15-16; 104:7), seen in the lightning flashes of divine judgment. In 43:16 the portrayal of the storm echoes earlier biblical depictions (Pss 18:8; 29:8), while the beautiful description of snow and frost (43:17-20) recalls Psalm 147:16-17. Sirach 43:22 speaks of the rain and dew that make the scorched land fertile (Ps 65:10-12).

[7]By it we know the sacred seasons
and pilgrimage feasts,
a light which wanes in its
course:
[8]The new moon like its name renews
itself;
how wondrous it is when it
changes:
A military signal for the waterskins
on high,
it paves the firmament with its
brilliance,
[9]The beauty of the heavens and the
glory of the stars,
a shining ornament in the
heights of God.
[10]By the LORD's command the moon
keeps its appointed place,
and does not fade as the stars
keep watch.
[11]Behold the rainbow! Then bless its
Maker,
for majestic indeed is its splendor;
[12]It spans the heavens with its glory,
the hand of God has stretched it
out in power.

[13]His rebuke marks out the path for
the hail,
and makes the flashes of his
judgment shine forth.
[14]For his own purposes he opens
the storehouse
and makes the rain clouds fly
like vultures.
[15]His might gives the clouds their
strength,
and breaks off the hailstones.
[16]The thunder of his voice makes
the earth writhe;
by his power he shakes the
mountains.
[17]A word from him drives on the
south wind,
whirlwind, hurricane, and
stormwind.
He makes the snow fly like birds;
it settles down like swarms of
locusts.

In 43:23-26, the sage turns to the sea, which the ancient Israelites regarded as terrifying (Ps 107:23-32; Jonah 1:4-16). God's might is evident in God's victory over the ocean's destructive power (Pss 29:3; 89:10-11), especially in the subsiding of the great flood (Gen 8:1-3). Sea voyagers tell of God's marvels that they have witnessed, such as the marine creatures (Ps 107:23-24). Each created being is like a messenger that obediently does God's will (Ps 104:4).

After these descriptions of God's marvelous creatures, Ben Sira turns to praising the Creator (43:27-33). Like Ecclesiastes 12:13, his summary is simple: God is the "all," in other words, the source of all that exists. One of the Dead Sea Scrolls praises God similarly: "Blessed is he who is everything" (4Q267 18.5.9). Ben Sira is not equating God with the created world, since "greater is he than all his works" (43:28). Human beings can praise God only inadequately for God's unfathomable greatness (Pss 106:2; 145:3). However, God does grant wisdom to the devout, some of whom will be celebrated in Sirach 44–50.

¹⁸Its shining whiteness blinds the
eyes,
the mind marvels at its steady
fall.
¹⁹He scatters frost like salt;
it shines like blossoms on the
thornbush.
²⁰He sends cold northern blasts
that harden the ponds like solid
ground,
Spreads a crust over every body of
water,
and clothes each pool with a
coat of armor.
²¹When mountain growth is scorched
by heat,
and flowering plains as by fire,
²²The dripping clouds restore them
all,
and the scattered dew enriches
the parched land.
²³His is the plan that calms the deep,
and plants the islands in the sea.

²⁴Those who go down to the sea
recount its extent,
and when we hear them we are
thunderstruck;
²⁵In it are his creatures, stupendous,
amazing,
all kinds of life, and the monsters
of the deep.
²⁶For him each messenger succeeds,
and at his bidding accomplishes
his will.

²⁷More than this we need not add; ▷
let the last word be, he is the all!
²⁸Let us praise him the more, since ▷
we cannot fathom him,
for greater is he than all his
works;
²⁹Awesome indeed is the LORD,
and wonderful his power.
³⁰Lift up your voices to glorify the
LORD
as much as you can, for there is
still more.

44:1–50:24 Praise of Israel's ancestors

Ben Sira's longest composition is a review of Israel's history, extending
from the Genesis patriarchs to the contemporary high priest Simeon the
Just. Whereas earlier biblical writers had praised God for acting through
figures like Moses, Aaron, and David (Pss 77:21; 144:10), Ben Sira actually
praises the illustrious figures themselves. This kind of hero list, paralleled
in later biblical books (1 Macc 2:51-60: Heb 11:4-38), is patterned on the
Greek encomium that mostly celebrated the deeds of male figures. This fact
may explain Ben Sira's exclusion of leading female figures from his composition, a serious omission for modern readers.

The whole poem consists of four sections. The introduction (44:1-15) is
followed by a longer section focusing particularly on the leading Penta-
teuchal figures with whom God made a covenant (44:16–45:26), ending
with a doxology (45:25-26). The next major section treats figures from
Israel's historical and prophetic books, especially prophets and kings (46:1–
49:16). The poem is completed by the praise of the recent high priest Simeon
(50:1-24), ending with a second doxology (50:22-24).

123

"Behold the rainbow! Then bless its Maker, for majestic indeed is its splendor" (Sir 43:11).

Extol him with renewed strength,
  do not grow weary, for you
    cannot fathom him.
³¹For who has seen him and can
    describe him?
  Who can praise him as he is?
³²Beyond these, many things lie
    hidden;
  only a few of his works have I
    seen.
³³It is the LORD who has made all
    things;
  to those who fear him he gives
    wisdom.

Praise of Israel's Great Ancestors

44 ¹I will now praise the godly,
  our ancestors, in their own
    time,
²The abounding glory of the Most
    High's portion,
  his own part, since the days of
    old.

³Subduers of the land in kingly
    fashion,
  renowned for their might,
Counselors in their prudence,
  seers of all things in prophecy,
⁴Resolute princes of the flock,
  lawgivers and their rules,
Sages skilled in composition,
  authors of sharp proverbs,
⁵Composers of melodious psalms,
  writers of lyric poems;
⁶Stalwart, solidly established,
  at peace in their own estates—
⁷All these were glorious in their
    time,
  illustrious in their day.
⁸Some of them left behind a name
  so that people recount their
    praises.
⁹Of others no memory remains,
  for when they perished, they
    perished,
As if they had never lived,

44:1-15 Praising unnamed heroes of faith

The Praise of the Ancestors begins with an introduction, sometimes used for services commemorating the deceased. Whereas the following sections name specific biblical characters, 44:1-15 offers a general celebration of the dead. The opening words of 44:1 echo the initial phrase of the poem extolling God's works in creation (42:15). The "Most High's portion" from ancient times denotes the people of Israel (Deut 32:7-9). Among the categories of important figures listed in 44:3-6, priests seem to be absent, though they play a prominent role later on (45:6-26; 50:1-24).

While all these figures were honored in their generation (44:7), some of them have left a reputation (particularly in the biblical narratives), whereas others have left no memorial (44:9). Since he lacks a clear belief in the afterlife (7:17; 17:27-28), Ben Sira wants Israel's heroes kept alive in the memory of their descendants (44:10-15). Accordingly, his characteristic emphasis is on surviving death through one's "name," either with a lasting "reputation" (39:9-11; 41:11-13), or with offspring carrying on the family "name" (16:4; 40:19).

they and their children after them.

¹⁰Yet these also were godly;
their virtues have not been forgotten.

¹¹Their wealth remains in their families,
their heritage with their descendants.

¹²Through God's covenant their family endures,
and their offspring for their sake.

¹³And for all time their progeny will endure,
their glory will never be blotted out;

¹⁴Their bodies are buried in peace,
but their name lives on and on.

¹⁵At gatherings their wisdom is retold,
and the assembly proclaims their praises.

The Early Ancestors

¹⁶[ENOCH walked with the LORD and was taken,
that succeeding generations might learn by his example.]

¹⁷NOAH, found just and perfect,
renewed the race in the time of devastation.
Because of his worth there were survivors,
and with a sign to him the deluge ended.

¹⁸A lasting covenant was made with him,
that never again would all flesh be destroyed.

¹⁹ABRAHAM, father of many peoples,
kept his glory without stain:

²⁰He observed the Most High's command,
and entered into a covenant with him;

44:16-23 The patriarchs of Genesis

After the introduction, the first part of the Praise of the Ancestors celebrates the Genesis patriarchs. The reference to Enoch in 44:16 (echoing Gen 5:24) may not be original, since this verse is absent from the Masada Hebrew text, and Enoch is also mentioned in 49:14. The Cairo Genizah Hebrew text depicts Enoch here as a sign of knowledge; in other words, a recipient of heavenly secrets (1 Enoch 92:1), whereas the Greek text portrays Enoch as an example of repentance (Wis 4:10-11). To accommodate both senses, the New American Bible offers a paraphrase in 44:16.

Sirach 44:17-23 deals with Noah, Abraham, Isaac, and Jacob, four patriarchs with whom God made or renewed a covenant (Gen 9:9; 17:9; 26:3-5; 28:13-15). Noah is celebrated for his role in enabling the human race to survive the flood (Gen 6:8–9:19; Heb 11:7). Sirach 44:17-18 links the cessation of the flood and God's covenant with Noah (Gen 9:9-11), while the rainbow is the sign that God will never again send a deluge on the entire earth (Gen 9:12-15).

Sirach 44:19-21 concerns Abraham (Gen 11:26–25:10). The sage alludes to the play on words in Genesis 17:4-5, whereby the patriarch's name was changed from Abram (exalted father) to Abraham (father of a multitude).

In his own flesh he incised the ordinance,
and when tested was found loyal.
[21]For this reason, God promised him
with an oath
to bless the nations through his
descendants,
To make him numerous as grains of
dust,
and to exalt his posterity like the
stars,
Giving them an inheritance from
sea to sea,
and from the River to the ends
of the earth.

[22]For ISAAC, too, he renewed the
same promise
because of Abraham, his father.

The covenant with all his forebears
was confirmed,
[23]and the blessing rested upon
the head of ISRAEL.
God acknowledged him as the firstborn,
and gave him his inheritance.
He fixed the boundaries for his
tribes
and their division into twelve.

Praise of Moses, Aaron, and Phinehas

45 [1]From him came the man
who would win the favor of all
the living:
Dear to God and human beings,
MOSES, whose memory is a
blessing.

Abraham is praised because his glory was unblemished, while in Hebrews 11:8-19 he appears as an example of faith. The covenant of Genesis 17:9-10 included the sign of circumcision, which is the "ordinance" in Abraham's flesh. In response to the severely testing command to offer his own son (Gen 22:1-2), Abraham was found faithful (Neh 9:8; 1 Macc 2:52). Accordingly, in Genesis 22:15-18 God made an oath to bless nations in his offspring.

In 44:22 Ben Sira mentions Isaac (Gen 21:1–35:29; Heb 11:20). The divine gift to him of a son was because of the promise of a great progeny made to Abraham (Gen 15:1-6; 17:4-8). Sirach 44:23 refers briefly to Isaac's son Jacob (Gen 25:20–49:33; Heb 11:21). The blessing came to rest on the head of Israel (Jacob), though he was younger than Esau, as a result of the trickery suggested by Rebekah (Gen 27:27-29). God gave Jacob his inheritance in terms of offspring, since his twelve sons became ancestors of tribes.

45:1-5 Moses

Chapter 45 considers three Levitical recipients of God's covenants (Moses, Aaron, Phinehas). According to the Hebrew text of 45:1, Jacob became the ancestor of Moses (*Moshe*), a man finding (*motse*) favor with everyone living. As a baby he found favor with Pharaoh's daughter (Exod 2:1-10). While the Greek version says that Moses resembled the angels in honor (45:2), the Hebrew manuscript asserts that Moses was honored like

²God made him like the angels in
   honor,
   and strengthened him with fear-
      ful powers.
³At his words God performed signs
   and sustained him in the king's
      presence.
He gave him the commandments
   for his people,
   and revealed to him his glory.
⁴Because of his trustworthiness and
      meekness
   God selected him from all flesh;
⁵He let him hear his voice,
   and led him into the cloud,
Where he handed over the com-
      mandments,
   the law of life and understanding,
That he might teach his precepts to
      Jacob,
   his judgments and decrees to
      Israel.

⁶He also raised up, like Moses in
      holiness,
   his brother AARON, of the tribe
      of Levi.
⁷He made his office perpetual
   and bestowed on him priesthood
      for his people;
He established him in honor
   and crowned him with lofty
      majesty.
⁸He clothed him in splendid gar-
      ments,
   and adorned him with glorious
      vestments:
Breeches, tunic, and robe
   ⁹with pomegranates at the hem
And a rustle of bells round about,
   whose pleasing sound at each
      step
Would make him heard within the
      sanctuary,
   a reminder for the people;

God, alluding to his God-like position toward Pharaoh, with Aaron as his mouthpiece (Exod 4:16; 7:1). The signs worked by Moses included the ten plagues (Exod 7:8–11:10), the exodus event (Exod 14:10-31), and the miracles in the wilderness (Exod 15:22–17:7). Though God's initial commands to Moses concerned the exodus (Exod 3:16-22), the lasting commandments were enshrined in the law (Exod 20:1–23:33). God's glory was also revealed to Moses, especially on Mount Sinai (Exod 24:16; 33:18).

Moses' trustworthiness toward God (45:4) was evident when most of the Israelites worshiped the golden calf (Exod 32:1-20). Although Moses accomplished great things, he was the meekest person on earth (Num 12:3), the most docile to the divine commands. God led him into the dark cloud of the storm-like theophany on Mount Sinai (Exod 19:16-19; 20:21). There God gave him the law of understanding and life (Deut 4:6; 30:15), so that he could teach it to the Israelites (Deut 4:14; Ps 147:19).

45:6-22 Aaron

Compared with Moses, Aaron receives more coverage here, because he more closely anticipates the high priest Simeon (50:1-21). The poem falls into two halves: Aaron's clothing (45:6-13) and his sacrifices (45:14-22). As

127

¹⁰The sacred vestments of gold, violet,
and crimson, worked with embroidery;
The breastpiece for decision, the ephod and cincture
¹¹with scarlet yarn, the work of the weaver;
Precious stones with seal engravings in golden settings, the work of the jeweler,
To commemorate in incised letters each of the tribes of Israel;
¹²On his turban a diadem of gold, its plate engraved with the sacred inscription—
Majestic, glorious, renowned for splendor,
a delight to the eyes, supremely beautiful.
¹³Before him, no one had been adorned with these,
nor may they ever be worn by any other
Except his sons and them alone, generation after generation, for all time.
¹⁴His grain offering is wholly burnt as an established offering twice each day;
¹⁵For Moses ordained him and anointed him with the holy oil,
In a lasting covenant with him and his family,
as permanent as the heavens,
That he should serve God in the priesthood
and bless the people in his name.
¹⁶He chose him from all the living to sacrifice burnt offerings and choice portions,
To burn incense, sweet odor as a memorial,

---

the first Israelite priest at the time of the exodus (Exod 28:1), Aaron was just as holy as his brother Moses (Ps 106:16).

Sirach 45:6-13 describes Aaron's glory, which consisted in worshiping God in splendid priestly attire according to the perpetual ordinance (Exod 28:2; 29:9). Sirach 45:8-9 portrays the high priest's robes (Exod 28:31-43), which had woven pomegranate shapes and gold bells attached to the hem. The "breastpiece for decision" (45:10) had a pocket containing the sacred lots of Urim and Thummim that were cast to discover God's will in doubtful matters (Exod 28:30). The ephod was a priestly garment like an apron (Exod 28:6-14), while the cincture or sash kept the tunic in place (Exod 28:39; Lev 8:7). On the breastpiece were twelve precious stones, each inscribed with the name of one of the Israelite tribes (Exod 28:17-21; Wis 18:24), while the miter or turban had a gold diadem (Exod 28:36). These high-priestly garments were meant for Aaron and his descendants only (Exod 29:4-9).

The rest of the passage (45:14-22) focuses on the sacrifices offered by Aaron, starting with the grain offering (Lev 6:13-16) that accompanied the regular Tamid sacrifice each morning and evening (Num 28:3-6). Moses ordained Aaron (Exod 28:41; 29:9) by anointing him with sacred oil (Exod

and to atone for the people of
Israel.
[17]He gave to him the laws,
and authority to prescribe and
to judge:
To teach precepts to the people,
and judgments to the Israelites.
[18]Strangers rose in anger against
him,
grew jealous of him in the
desert—
The followers of Dathan and Abiram,
and the band of Korah in their
defiance.
[19]When the LORD saw this he became
angry,
and destroyed them in his burning wrath.
He brought against them a marvel,
and consumed them in flaming
fire.
[20]Then he increased the glory of
Aaron

and bestowed upon him his
inheritance:
The sacred offerings he allotted to
him,
with the showbread as his portion;
[21]The oblations of the LORD are his
food,
a gift to him and his descendants.
[22]But he holds no land among the
people
nor shares with them their heritage;
For the LORD himself is his portion
and inheritance
among the Israelites.

[23]PHINEHAS too, the son of Eleazar,
was the courageous third of his
line
When, zealous for the God of all,
he met the crisis of his people
And, at the prompting of his noble
heart,

30:30-33). Aaron's tasks included giving the high-priestly blessing (Lev 9:22), offering sacrifices (Lev 2:2), and atoning for the people's sins (Lev 16:32-34). The priests had the role of judging legal cases (Deut 17:8-11) and of instructing the people (Lev 10:11; Deut 33:10). Sirach 45:18-19 alludes to the rebellion of Korah, Dathan, and Abiram, who challenged the unique holiness of Aaron and Moses (Num 16:3). The "marvel" (45:19) was the sudden sinking of the ground that swallowed up the rebels, along with the sudden fire that came from the sanctuary to destroy their supporters (Num 16:31-35).

According to 45:20, Aaron's glory was increased by the allocation of Levites to assist the priests, and by the grant of the priestly share of the sacrifices (Lev 24:5-9; Num 18:6-19). Yet because God was their inheritance, the priests would not inherit any land (Num 18:20).

45:23-26 Phinehas

The zealous priest Phinehas, Aaron's grandson, receives almost as much coverage as Moses. During a time of apostasy, Phinehas killed an Israelite

atoned for the children of Israel.
²⁴Therefore, on him also God con-
ferred the right,
in a covenant of friendship, to
provide for the sanctuary,
So that he and his descendants
should possess the high priesthood forever.
²⁵For even his covenant with David,
the son of Jesse of the tribe of
Judah,
Was an individual heritage through
one son alone;
but the heritage of Aaron is for
all his descendants.

So now bless the LORD
who has crowned you with glory!

²⁶May he grant you wisdom of heart
to govern his people in justice,
Lest the benefits you confer should
be forgotten,
or your authority, throughout all
time.

Joshua, Caleb, the Judges, and Samuel

46 ¹Valiant warrior was JOSHUA,
son of Nun,
aide to Moses in the prophetic
office,
Formed to be, as his name implies,
the great savior of God's chosen
ones,
To punish the enemy
and to give to Israel their heritage.

who had taken a Midianite wife and was engaged in the worship of Baal (Num 25:6-13; Ps 106:30-31). The risk was that the Israelites would be led into pagan practices. According to 45:23, Phinehas's zealous action atoned for Israelite iniquity (1 Macc 2:26). As a reward, he received an eternal covenant, not only to care for the sanctuary, but also to have the high priesthood forever among his descendants (Num 25:12-13; 1 Macc 2:54).

Sirach 45:25 refers to God's covenant with Aaron, contrasted with the Davidic covenant (Ps 89:29-30; 1 Macc 2:57). David's royal line ceased to provide a king for Israel during the Babylonian exile (2 Chr 36:11-19), whereas the high-priestly line still provided Israel with a religious leader (50:1-24). The concluding doxology (45:25-26) is briefer than the one in 50:22-24. According to Ben Sira, if the new priestly leadership after Simeon's death leads the people wisely, their name will live on for generations (44:10-15). Sadly, Simeon's descendants did not maintain the traditional fidelity he had shown toward Israel's God (2 Macc 4:7).

46:1-12 Joshua, Caleb, and the judges

Sirach 46:1 praises Joshua as a warrior (Josh 10:7–11:23) and as Moses' servant (Num 11:28). Using a Hebrew wordplay, Ben Sira notes that Joshua (*Jehoshua*) brought about great salvation (*teshuah*) for the Israelites (1 Macc 2:55). Joshua's task involved both dealing vengeance to Israel's enemies

²What glory was his when he raised
his hand,
to brandish his sword against
the city!
³Who could withstand him
when he fought the battles of
the LORD?
⁴Was it not by that same hand the
sun stopped,
so that one day became two?
⁵He called upon the Most High
God
when his enemies beset him on
all sides,
And God Most High answered him
with hailstones of tremendous
power,

⁶That rained down upon the hostile
army
till on the slope he destroyed the
foe;
That all the doomed nations might
know
the LORD was watching over his
people's battles.
He was indeed a devoted follower
of God
⁷and showed himself loyal in
Moses' lifetime.
He and CALEB, son of Jephunneh,
when they opposed the rebel
assembly,
Averted God's anger from the
people

(Josh 10:13) and giving Israel their inheritance (Deut 1:38; Josh 11:23). For modern readers, shocked by the destruction of indigenous peoples, the Bible's praise of Joshua is problematic. In the ancient world, however, his warfare to provide a homeland for his refugee people would have been regarded as natural. Sirach 46:2-3 praises Joshua for brandishing his sword against the city of Ai (Josh 8:18-26) and for fighting God's battles (Josh 1:9; 1 Sam 18:17). In 46:4-6 Ben Sira celebrates Joshua's victory at Gibeon, when the sun stood still at his command, while the enemy was struck with hailstones (Josh 10:7-14).

Joshua is praised because, like Caleb, he fully followed after God (Josh 14:8-9). Significantly (46:7), both men opposed the other Israelite spies who made the people afraid to enter the promised land (Num 14:6; 1 Macc 2:56). As a reward, only these two (out of six hundred thousand) were allowed to enter the land (Num 14:22-38; Josh 14:6-13). Caleb's family gained a heritage of high ground at Hebron (Josh 15:13-14).

The brief treatment of the judges (46:11-12) praises only those who did not turn away from God; thus, for instance, Samson is probably excluded. It seems that only the minor judges deserve praise (Judg 10:1-5; 12:8-15), since they had offspring and proper burial. Sirach 46:12 wishes that their bones may sprout afresh from their burial place (49:10). Since the sage has no belief in the afterlife (14:16; 41:4), he is praying that worthy successors may continue the judges' good reputation on earth.

and suppressed the wicked
complaint.
⁸Because of this, these two alone
were spared
from the six hundred thousand
infantry,
To lead the people into their heritage,
the land flowing with milk and
honey.
⁹The strength God gave to Caleb
remained with him even in old
age
Till he won his way onto the summits
of the land;
his family too received a heritage,
¹⁰That all the offspring of Jacob
might know
how good it is to be a devoted
follower of the LORD.

¹¹The JUDGES, each one of them,
whose hearts were not deceived,
Who did not abandon God—
may their memory be ever
blessed!
¹²May their bones flourish with new
life where they lie,
and their names receive fresh
luster in their children!
¹³Beloved of his people, dear to his
Maker,
pledged in a vow from his
mother's womb,
As one consecrated to the LORD in
the prophetic office,
was SAMUEL, the judge who
offered sacrifice.
At God's word he established the
kingdom
and anointed princes to rule the
people.
¹⁴By the law of the LORD he judged
the congregation,
and visited the encampments of
Jacob.
¹⁵As a trustworthy prophet he was
sought out
and his words proved him to be
a true seer.
¹⁶He, too, called upon the mighty
Lord
when his enemies pressed him
on every side,
and offered up a suckling lamb.

46:13-20 Samuel

Like Moses in 45:1, Samuel was esteemed by God and humanity (1 Sam 2:26). After noting that Samuel was pledged in a vow from his mother's womb (1 Sam 1:27-28), Sirach 46:13 refers to his anointing of Israel's first two kings, Saul and David (1 Sam 10:1; 16:13). Ben Sira then praises Samuel for his reliability as a seer (1 Sam 3:20; 9:9). Sirach 46:16-18 recalls the battle with the Philistines at Mizpah (1 Sam 7:7-13), when Samuel offered sacrifice to God, who responded by granting victory to the Israelites. Ben Sira also refers to the dying Samuel's testimony that he was innocent of any wrong-doing against the Israelites (1 Sam 12:3). The final verse speaks of Saul's consultation of the witch of Endor (1 Sam 28:8-19), against the biblical prohibition (Lev 19:31; Deut 18:10-11). The text depicts the dead Samuel as speaking from the grave, prophesying Saul's death in battle (1 Sam 28:13-19).

¹⁷Then the LORD thundered from
    heaven,
  and the tremendous roar of his
      voice was heard.
¹⁸He brought low the rulers of the
    enemy
  and destroyed all the lords of
      the Philistines.
¹⁹When Samuel neared the end of
    life,
  he testified before the LORD and
      his anointed prince,
  "No bribe or secret gift have I taken
      from anyone!"
  and no one could accuse him.
²⁰Even after death his guidance was
    sought;
  he made known to the king his
      fate.
From the grave he spoke in
    prophecy
  to put an end to wickedness.

Nathan, David, and Solomon

47 ¹After him came NATHAN
    who served in David's pres-
        ence.
²Like the choice fat of sacred offer-
    ings,
  so was DAVID in Israel.
³He played with lions as though
    they were young goats,
  and with bears, like lambs of the
      flock.
⁴As a youth he struck down the giant
  and wiped out the people's dis-
      grace;
His hand let fly the slingstone
  that shattered the pride of
      Goliath.
⁵For he had called upon the Most
    High God,
  who gave strength to his right
      arm
To defeat the skilled warrior

47:1-11 David

This poem praises King David for winning battles and providing music for divine worship. Ben Sira first mentions the prophet Nathan, whose oracle promised eternal sovereignty to the Davidic line (2 Sam 7:4-17). Sirach 47:2 then likens the king to choice fat from the temple offerings (Lev 4:8-10). Next Ben Sira celebrates David's courage, which enabled him to play with lions and bears (1 Sam 17:34-36; Isa 11:6-7), as well as to defeat Goliath with a sling stone (1 Sam 17:48-51). According to 47:5, David's victory over the Philistine warrior resulted from God's help (1 Sam 17:45-47). Then the Israelite womenfolk sang songs praising David for achieving far more than Saul (1 Sam 18:7; 21:12). When David began his reign, he subdued the surrounding enemies, such as the Philistines (2 Sam 5:17-25). As a result of David's campaigning, the Philistines never again posed a major threat to Israel (2 Chr 17:11; 26:6-7).

Amid his military successes (47:8), David devoutly gave praise to God Most High (Pss 9:2; 34:2). In fact, the Hebrew Psalter associates seventy-three psalms with David. Sirach 47:8-10 depicts David having musical melodies sung before the altar at the temporary sanctuary, before the build-

and establish the might of his
people.
⁶Therefore the women sang his
praises
and honored him for "the tens
of thousands."
When he received the royal crown,
he battled
⁷and subdued the enemy on
every side.
He campaigned against the hostile
Philistines
and shattered their power till
our own day.
⁸With his every deed he offered
thanks
to God Most High, in words of
praise.
With his whole heart he loved his
Maker
⁹and daily had his praises sung;
¹⁰He added beauty to the feasts

and solemnized the seasons of
each year
⁹ᵇWith string music before the altar,
providing sweet melody for the
psalms
¹⁰ᵇSo that when the Holy Name was
praised,
before daybreak the sanctuary
would resound.
¹¹The LORD forgave him his sins
and exalted his strength forever;
He conferred on him the rights of
royalty
and established his throne in
Israel.

¹²Because of his merits he had as
successor
a wise son, who lived in security:
¹³SOLOMON reigned during an era of
peace,
for God brought rest to all his
borders.

---

ing of the temple by his son Solomon (1 Chr 22:6). This echoes the Chronicler's tradition that David provided musicians to praise God at the sanctuary (1 Chr 16:4-42; 25:1-7).

In 47:11 the sage alludes indirectly to David's murder of Uriah and adultery with Bathsheba (2 Sam 11) by mentioning that God removed his transgression (2 Sam 12:13; Ps 51:1-4). Accordingly, he figures among Judah's three righteous kings in 49:4. David's strength was exalted "forever," because of the promise of eternal sovereignty to his offspring (2 Sam 7:16; 1 Macc 2:57). Christians see Jesus as fulfilling that promise (Luke 1:32-33).

47:12-25 Solomon and his successors

Ben Sira notes Solomon's great achievements as temple builder and mouthpiece of wisdom, as well as the harmful effects of his marriages to pagan wives. Sirach 47:12 introduces Solomon as David's wise son (1 Kgs 5:21), who reigned in a time of security (1 Kgs 5:5). God had granted Solomon "rest" (1 Kgs 5:18), as a result of his father David's military campaigns (2 Sam 7:1). Solomon constructed a house (= temple) to God's name (2 Sam 7:13; 1 Kgs 8:15-21), intended to last forever (Ps 78:69).

He built a house to the name of God,
and established a lasting sanctuary.
[14]How wise you were when you
were young,
overflowing with instruction,
like the Nile in flood!
[15]Your understanding covered the
whole earth,
and, like a sea, filled it with
knowledge.
[16]Your fame reached distant coasts,
and you were beloved for your
peaceful reign.
[17]With song and proverb and riddle,
and with your answers, you
astounded the nations.
[18]You were called by that glorious
name
which was conferred upon
Israel.

Gold you gathered like so much iron;
you heaped up silver as though
it were lead.
[19]But you abandoned yourself to
women
and gave them dominion over
your body.
[20]You brought a stain upon your
glory,
shame upon your marriage bed,
Wrath upon your descendants,
and groaning upon your deathbed.
[21]Thus two governments came into
being,
when in Ephraim kingship was
usurped.
[22]But God does not withdraw his
mercy,
nor permit even one of his
promises to fail.

Sirach 47:14 celebrates Solomon's youthful wisdom, granted in answer to his prayer soon after his accession (1 Kgs 3:7-9). Indeed, his wisdom was famous far and wide (1 Kgs 10:24; Matt 12:42). Sirach 47:17 alludes to the biblical statement that Solomon uttered proverbs and songs (1 Kgs 5:12), while Proverbs 1:6 attributes riddles to him. Solomon's glorious name was "Jedidiah" (2 Sam 12:25), meaning "beloved of the Lord." Ben Sira also notes Solomon's amassing of abundant wealth in precious metals (1 Kgs 10:25-27), contrary to the Torah (Deut 17:17).

Despite his wisdom (47:19), he allowed his love of foreign women to lead him into idolatry (1 Kgs 11:1-13). As in 9:2, critics have noted a misogynistic tone here, when Ben Sira disparages Solomon for letting "women" rule over his body (Prov 31:3). While the book of Kings blames Solomon's idolatry for the breakup of the kingdom (1 Kgs 11:9-11), Ben Sira focuses more specifically on his liaisons with foreign women.

Sirach 47:21 refers to the end of the united monarchy immediately after Solomon's death (1 Kgs 12:1-24). However, 47:22 asserts that despite Solomon's sin, God did not abandon the covenant loyalty, but fulfilled the promise by providing a descendant for David on the throne (2 Sam 7:15; Ps 89:34-38).

He does not uproot the posterity of the chosen,
nor destroy the offspring of his friends.
So he gave to Jacob a remnant,
to David a root from his own family.

Rehoboam and Jeroboam

²³Solomon finally slept with his ancestors,
and left behind him one of his sons,
Broad in folly, narrow in sense,
whose policy made the people rebel.
Then arose the one who should not be remembered,
the sinner who led Israel into sin,

Who brought ruin to Ephraim
²⁴and caused them to be exiled from their land.

Elijah and Elisha

²⁵Their sinfulness grew more and more,
and they gave themselves to every evil

48 ¹Until like fire a prophet appeared,
his words a flaming furnace.
²The staff of life, their bread, he shattered,
and in his zeal he made them few in number.
³By God's word he shut up the heavens

Unlike his father Solomon, Rehoboam lacked sense (47:23). He drove the Israelites into rebellion by imposing heavier taxation on them (1 Kgs 12:1-19), allowing "the sinner" (Jeroboam, son of Nebat) to lead the Israelite tribes astray. Jeroboam's sin was to set up golden calves at Dan and Bethel, so that the people would worship there rather than at Jerusalem (1 Kgs 12:26-30). According to 2 Kings 17:21-23, this sin of idolatry ultimately caused the northern Israelites to be exiled by the Assyrians in 722 B.C.

48:1-16 Elijah and Elisha

Sirach 48:1 aptly compares Elijah to fire, recalling the prophet's zealous temperament (1 Kgs 19:14; 1 Macc 2:58), the way he brought down "fire" (= lightning) from heaven (48:3), and the effect of his words like a burning furnace (Mal 3:19). Then 48:2 refers to his calling of a prolonged drought (1 Kgs 17:1; Jas 5:17), causing famine for Israel (1 Kgs 18:2; Luke 4:25). In 48:3 Ben Sira mentions three bolts of lightning that Elijah brought down from the sky; the first fell on the offerings at Mount Carmel (1 Kgs 18:38), while the second and third killed the messengers sent by King Ahab's son Ahaziah (2 Kgs 1:9-14). One of the prophet's awesome deeds was to restore to life the son of the widow of Zarephath (1 Kgs 17:22).

Sirach 48:6 recalls that Elijah foretold King Ahab's death as a punishment for his judicial murder of Naboth (1 Kgs 21:19; 22:34-38). The prophet

and three times brought down fire.

⁴How awesome are you, ELIJAH!
Whose glory is equal to yours?
⁵You brought a dead body back to life
from Sheol, by the will of the LORD.
⁶You sent kings down to destruction,
and nobles, from their beds of sickness.
⁷You heard threats at Sinai,
at Horeb avenging judgments.
⁸You anointed the agent of these punishments,
the prophet to succeed in your place.
⁹You were taken aloft in a whirlwind,
in a chariot with fiery horses.
¹⁰You are destined, it is written, in time to come
to put an end to wrath before the day of the LORD,

To turn back the hearts of parents toward their children,
and to re-establish the tribes of Israel.
¹¹Blessed is the one who shall have seen you before he dies!

¹²When Elijah was enveloped in the whirlwind,
ELISHA was filled with his spirit;
He worked twice as many marvels,
and every utterance of his mouth was wonderful.
During his lifetime he feared no one,
nor was anyone able to intimidate his will.
¹³Nothing was beyond his power;
and from where he lay buried,
his body prophesied.
¹⁴In life he performed wonders,
and after death, marvelous deeds.
¹⁵Despite all this the people did not repent,

---

also predicted the injured King Ahaziah's death, as the penalty for his worship of Baal (2 Kgs 1:16-17). The avenging judgments heard by the prophet on Mount Horeb were against the apostate Israelites (1 Kgs 19:17). To inflict this vengeance, Elijah selected two kings (1 Kgs 19:15-17), Jehu to unleash a violent campaign against Ahab's son Joram (2 Kgs 9:14-26), and Hazael to cause the death of the Syrian king Ben-hadad (2 Kgs 8:14-15). The prophetic successor anointed by Elijah was Elisha (1 Kgs 19:16).

Like Enoch (49:14), Elijah was taken up to heaven (48:9). The prophet's assumption took place in a whirlwind (2 Kgs 2:11; 1 Macc 2:58), when Elisha saw the fiery horses and chariot. Elijah's future role, written in Malachi 3:23-24, was to put an end to wrath before the final judgment and reconcile parents and children (Matt 17:10; Luke 1:17). The role of reestablishing Israel's tribes echoes the task of God's servant in Isaiah 49:6. The damaged Hebrew manuscript of 48:11 may allude to Elisha, who saw Elijah ascending to heaven (2 Kgs 2:9-12), or else to those who will be alive at Elijah's return to earth (Mal 3:23). However, the Greek version of 48:11 introduces the idea of the afterlife: "Blessed are those who have seen you, and those who have fallen asleep in love, for we too shall certainly live."

nor did they give up their sins,
Until they were uprooted from their
land
and scattered all over the earth.

Judah

But Judah remained, a tiny people,
with its ruler from the house of
David.
¹⁶Some of them did what was right,
but others were extremely sinful.

Hezekiah and Isaiah

¹⁷HEZEKIAH fortified his city
and had water brought into it;
With bronze tools he cut through
the rocks
and dammed up a mountain site
for water.
¹⁸During his reign Sennacherib led
an invasion
and sent his adjutant;
He shook his fist at Zion
and blasphemed God in his
pride.
¹⁹The people's hearts melted within
them,
and they were in anguish like
that of childbirth.
²⁰But they called upon the Most
High God
and lifted up their hands to him;
He heard the prayer they uttered,
and saved them through ISAIAH.

Endowed with a double share of Elijah's spirit (2 Kgs 2:9), his successor Elisha performed twice as many miracles (48:12). Thus, whereas Elijah raised the son of the widow of Zarephath (1 Kgs 17:17-24), Elisha raised two persons, the Shunammite woman's son and the corpse thrown into Elisha's grave (2 Kgs 4:32-37; 13:21). The latter event is the subject of 48:13. Because the Israelites in the northern kingdom did not repent despite Elisha's miracles, they were eventually punished by being removed from their land and scattered throughout the Near East (2 Kgs 17:6-12). By contrast, a remnant was left to Judah (Isa 1:8-9). Whereas some of the Judean kings practiced uprightness (such as Hezekiah and Josiah), others (such as Manasseh) were very wicked.

48:17-25 Hezekiah and Isaiah

In praising the good king Hezekiah, Ben Sira first mentions his building work in Jerusalem (as with Nehemiah in 49:13), because such work foreshadowed the achievements of the high priest Simeon (50:1-4) in the sage's own lifetime. Sirach 48:17 makes a Hebrew wordplay on Hezekiah's name: he "fortified" (*hizzak*) his city and also brought water into its midst (2 Kgs 20:20). Next the sage describes Sennacherib's siege of Jerusalem in 701 B.C., mentioning the taunts of the Assyrian commander, the Jerusalemites' fear, the prayer of Hezekiah, and Isaiah's promise of deliverance (2 Kgs 18:13–19:34; Isa 36:1–38:22). Whereas 2 Kings 19:35 attributes sudden death in the

²¹God struck the camp of the
    Assyrians
    and routed them with a plague.
²²For Hezekiah did what was right
    and held fast to the paths of
    David,
As ordered by the illustrious prophet
Isaiah, who saw truth in visions.
²³In his lifetime he turned back the
    sun
    and prolonged the life of the king.
²⁴By his powerful spirit he looked
    into the future
    and consoled the mourners of
    Zion;
²⁵He foretold what would happen
    till the end of time,
    hidden things yet to be fulfilled.

Josiah and the Prophets

49 ¹The name JOSIAH is like blended
    incense,
    made lasting by a skilled per-
    fumer.
Precious is his memory, like honey
    to the taste,
    like music at a banquet.
²For he grieved over our betrayals,
    and destroyed the abominable
    idols.
³He kept his heart fixed on God,
    and in times of lawlessness
    practiced virtue.
⁴Except for David, Hezekiah, and
    Josiah,
    they all were wicked;

Assyrian camp to the angel of the Lord, 48:21 ascribes it to a plague or epidemic. Sirach 48:22 recalls Isaiah's role in the cure of Hezekiah, along with the associated sign of the shadow's movement on a royal staircase (2 Kgs 20:1-11). Finally the sage refers to Isaiah's visions of the future and his promise of comfort for the mourners in Zion (2 Kgs 20:17; Isa 61:1-3).

49:1-13 From Josiah to Nehemiah

King Josiah (640–609 B.C.) ruled Jerusalem shortly before the Babylonian exile. He was a great religious reformer, because in his reign the law of Moses was rediscovered (2 Kgs 22:8). Accordingly, Josiah's name is compared to blended incense—an appropriate image because of his restoration of temple worship (Exod 30:7). Josiah's grief over Judah's betrayals of God was clear from his penitent reaction to the reading of the Torah scroll (2 Kgs 22:11) and from his subsequent destruction of idols that had even been placed in the temple (2 Kgs 23:4-14).

Ben Sira's verdict on Judah's monarchy (49:4) echoes the view of the books of Kings (2 Kgs 18:3; 23:25). Only David, Hezekiah, and Josiah are judged to have been God-fearing, since all the others tolerated idolatry in their kingdom (including Solomon, according to 1 Kgs 11:5-6). Indeed, the Bible regards the Babylonian exile as divine punishment of the people for disobeying the commandments (2 Chr 36:15-21). Sirach 49:5-6 refers to the events of 587 B.C., when a "foreign nation" (the Babylonians) burned Jerusalem (2 Kgs 25:9).

They abandoned the Law of the
Most High,
these kings of Judah, right to the
very end.
⁵So he gave over their power to
others,
their glory to a foreign nation
⁶Who burned the holy city
and left its streets desolate,
⁷As foretold by JEREMIAH. They mis-
treated him
who even in the womb had been
made a prophet,
To root out, pull down, and destroy,
and then to build and to plant.
⁸EZEKIEL beheld a vision
and described the different creatures of the chariot;
⁹He also referred to JOB,
who always persevered in the
right path.

¹⁰Then, too, the TWELVE PROPHETS—
may their bones flourish with
new life where they lie!—
They gave new strength to Jacob
and saved him with steadfast
hope.

The Heroes After the Exile

¹¹How to extol ZERUBBABEL?
He was like a signet ring on the
right hand,
¹²And JESHUA, Jozadak's son?
In their time they rebuilt the
altar
And erected the holy temple,
destined for everlasting glory.
¹³Exalted be the memory of
NEHEMIAH!
He rebuilt our ruined walls,
Restored our shattered defenses,
and set up gates and bars.

Sirach 49:7 notes that Jeremiah had been called as a prophet even in his mother's womb (Jer 1:5). His ministry involved both destruction and construction (Jer 1:10; 18:7-10), since he announced Jerusalem's downfall (Jer 7:14-15; 26:6-9) but also its future rebuilding (Jer 29:10-14; 30:17-18). Ben Sira then mentions Jeremiah's contemporary, Ezekiel, whose prophetic call included a vision of God in a heavenly chariot surrounded by various creatures (Ezek 1:4-21). Ezekiel also referred to Job as an example of a very righteous person (Ezek 14:14), famous for persevering in the right path (Job 2:10; Jas 5:11). Sirach 49:10 alludes to the twelve Minor Prophets (Hosea through Malachi), whose writings were collected into one book in Jewish tradition. As in 46:12, Ben Sira wishes that their bones may sprout afresh from their resting place (49:10); in other words, that worthy successors may continue their good work.

Passing quickly over the exilic period, Ben Sira mentions Israel's civil leader (Zerubbabel) and chief priest (Jeshua) in the early years after the people returned from Babylonian exile (49:11-12). The preciousness of Zerubbabel is indicated by the image of the signet ring (Hag 2:23). Both Zerubbabel and Jeshua (called Joshua in Hag 1:12 and Zech 3:1) were involved in the rebuilding of the Jerusalem temple, completed in 515 B.C.

The Earliest Patriarchs

¹⁴Few on earth have been created
like ENOCH;
he also was taken up bodily.
¹⁵Was ever a man born like JOSEPH?
Even his dead body was provided
for.
¹⁶Glorious, too, were SHEM and SETH
and ENOSH;
but beyond that of any living
being was the splendor
of ADAM.

Simeon, Son of Jochanan

50 ¹Greatest of his family, the glory
of his people,
was SIMEON the priest, son of
Jochanan,
In whose time the house of God
was renovated,
in whose days the temple was
reinforced.
²In his time also the retaining wall
was built
with powerful turrets for the
temple precincts.

(Ezra 3:2; 6:15). Sirach 49:13 praises Nehemiah, who came from Persia to Jerusalem around 445 B.C. to rebuild the city walls (Neh 2:1-18). Nehemiah's building activity foreshadows the construction works of the high priest Simeon (50:1-4). Strangely, Ben Sira omits the priestly scribe Ezra (Ezra 7:1-6).

49:14-16 Heroes of ancient time

Although Ben Sira began the Praise of the Ancestors with the early patriarchs in Genesis (44:17-23), he unexpectedly kept the earliest Genesis characters until last. Possibly he wished to close the circle of Israel's history, or else to highlight the comparison with Simeon the high priest in 50:1-24.

If the mention of Enoch in 44:16 is a later addition to the text, Ben Sira has deliberately left Enoch till the end (49:14), to downplay his importance as a recipient of divine revelation (as claimed in the book of Enoch). Instead, the sage merely refers to the tradition of Genesis 5:24 that he was taken by God into heaven (Heb 11:5). In 49:15 Ben Sira refers to Jacob's son Joseph, whose bones were carefully brought by the Israelites from Egypt to the promised land (Gen 50:25; Josh 24:32). Sirach 49:16 draws on Genesis 5:1-32 in its mention of three of Adam's descendants: Shem (Noah's son), Seth (brother of Cain and Abel), and Enosh (Seth's son). The most glorious living person was Adam, who initially shared in God's glory, before his sin and expulsion from the garden of Eden (Wis 10:1-2).

50:1-24 Simeon the high priest

Ben Sira's celebration of Simeon II, who had probably recently died, forms the culmination of the Praise of the Ancestors. Simeon (or Simon) was the high priest in Jerusalem at the end of the third century B.C. (approximately

³In his time the reservoir was dug,
a pool as vast as the sea.
⁴He protected the people against brigands
and strengthened the city against the enemy.
⁵How splendid he was as he looked out from the tent,
as he came from behind the veil!
⁶Like a star shining among the clouds,
like the full moon at the festal season;
⁷Like sun shining upon the temple of the King,
like a rainbow appearing in the cloudy sky;
⁸Like blossoms on the branches in springtime,
like a lily by running waters;
Like a green shoot on Lebanon in summer,
⁹like the fire of incense at sacrifice;
Like a vessel of hammered gold, studded with all kinds of precious stones;
¹⁰Like a luxuriant olive tree heavy with fruit,
a plant with branches abounding in oil;
¹¹Wearing his glorious robes,
and vested in sublime magnificence,

219–196). Since civil government was under the Greek-speaking rulers of Palestine, Simeon was a national figurehead, embodying aspects of Jewish political as well as religious leadership. Sirach 50:1-4 celebrates the high priest's building activities in Jerusalem. Like Jeshua son of Jozadak, he repaired the temple (49:12). Like Hezekiah and Nehemiah, he fortified the walls in Jerusalem (48:17; 49:13). Like Hezekiah, he had a reservoir for water dug (48:17).

Although many scholars have seen 50:5-21 as a description of the Day of Atonement, the details do not match Leviticus 16 or the Mishnaic tractate *Yoma*, and the portrayal is too florid for such a penitential day. Instead, the events generally correspond to the daily whole burnt offering or Tamid (Num 28–29; Mishnaic tractate *Tamid* 6.3–7.3). Even the high priest's exit from within the veil (50:5) need not refer to the Day of Atonement (the only day of the year when the high priest went inside the veil to the holy of holies, according to Lev 16:2), since another veil or curtain separated the court of the priests from the outer court.

Sirach 50:5-10 employs poetic imagery to depict the splendor of Simeon appearing for a public sacrifice. Comparison of the high priest with the stars, moon, sun, and rainbow recalls the sage's earlier hymn to the Creator (43:1-12). The likening of the high priest to trees and flowers parallels the portrayal of wisdom in an earlier poem (24:13-15). Fittingly, Ben Sira also compares Simeon to the incense fire (50:9), since the high priest would have

As he ascended the glorious altar
and lent majesty to the court of
the sanctuary.
¹²When he received the portions
from the priests
while he stood before the sacrificial wood,
His sons stood round him like a
garland,
like young cedars on Lebanon;
And like poplars by the brook they
surrounded him,
¹³all the sons of Aaron in their
glory,
With the offerings to the LORD in
their hands,
in the presence of the whole
assembly of Israel.

¹⁴Once he had completed the service
at the altar
and arranged the sacrificial
hearth for the Most High,
¹⁵And had stretched forth his hand
for the cup,
to offer blood of the grape,
And poured it out at the foot of the
altar,
a sweet-smelling odor to God
the Most High,
¹⁶Then the sons of Aaron would
sound a blast,
the priests, on their trumpets of
beaten metal;
A blast to resound mightily
as a reminder before the Most
High.

---

burned incense over the grain offering (Lev 2:1-2). The comparison of Simeon II to the luxuriant olive tree echoes Zechariah 4:11-14.

Sirach 50:11-21 describes the high priest's sacrificial service when (like Aaron in 45:8-12) he was dressed in magnificent robes (Exod 28:2-43) for officiating at the bronze altar in the court facing the sanctuary (Exod 27:1-2; 2 Chr 4:1). Sirach 50:14-15 reports the libation of wine, poured out at the foot of the altar (Num 15:5; 28:7), while 50:16 recounts the blast sounded on silver trumpets (Num 10:1-10). According to 50:17, the people fell prostrate in adoration (2 Chr 29:28-29). While the smoke of the sacrifice ascended, the temple singers offered hymns of praise (2 Chr 29:27), as decreed by King David (47:9-10). In an echo of Exodus 34:6, God was invoked as the "Merciful One." According to 50:20-21, the ceremony concluded with the high priest's blessing of the assembled crowd (Lev 9:22-23; Num 6:23-27), using the sacred name YAHWEH (here translated as LORD). In later tradition the high priest only pronounced the sacred name once a year on the Day of Atonement (*Mishnah Sanhedrin* 10.1), but this was not so in earliest times (2 Sam 6:18).

The poem on Simeon ends with a doxology (50:22-24), resembling the one in 45:25-26. On the basis of 50:22-24 Martin Rinkart (d. 1649) composed the hymn "Now Thank We All Our God." The sage's prayer in 50:23 is for wisdom for the sons of the high priest Simeon (Onias III and Jeshua). In the Hebrew text of 50:24 Ben Sira prays for Simeon's heirs, that God may

17All the people with one accord
    would fall with face to the ground
In adoration before the Most High,
    before the Holy One of Israel.

18Then hymns would re-echo,
    and over the throng sweet strains
    of praise resound.
19All the people of the land would
    shout for joy,
    praying to the Merciful One,
As the high priest completed the
    service at the altar
    by presenting to God the fitting
    sacrifice.
20Then coming down he would
    raise his hands
    over all the congregation of
    Israel;
The blessing of the LORD would be
    upon his lips,
    the name of the LORD would be
    his glory.

21The people would again fall down
    to receive the blessing of the
    Most High.

22And now, bless the God of all,
    who has done wonders on earth;
Who fosters growth from the womb,
    fashioning it according to his will!
23May he grant you a wise heart
    and abide with you in peace;
24May his goodness toward Simeon
    last forever;
    may he fulfill for him the cove-
    nant with Phinehas
So that it may not be abrogated for
    him
    or his descendants while the
    heavens last.

Epilogue

25My whole being loathes two
    nations,
    the third is not even a people:

---

permanently maintain for them the "covenant with Phinehas." According to this covenant of peace (Num 25:12-13), the divine promise was that the high priesthood would remain in the line of Phinehas forever (45:24). But with the murder of Onias III and the overthrow of his brother Jeshua, now called Jason (2 Macc 4:26, 34), Simeon II's priestly line came to an ignominious end. Hence, the grandson's Greek translation eliminated the covenant with Phinehas and updated 50:24 to match the situation of the late second century B.C.: "May his mercy remain faithful with us, and in our days may he redeem us."

POSTSCRIPTS AND APPENDICES

Sirach 50:25–51:30

50:25-29 Two postscripts

    The book's first postscript (50:25-26) records the sage's bitter attack on three neighboring nations: the Idumeans (formerly Edomites) to the south and east of Judea (2 Macc 10:14-17); the Hellenized inhabitants of the western coastal region inhabited formerly by the Philistines (1 Macc 5:68); and

²⁶The inhabitants of Seir and
  Philistia,
and the foolish people who dwell
  in Shechem.

²⁷Wise instruction, appropriate
  proverbs,
I have written in this book—
I, Yeshua Ben Eleazar Ben Sira—
  as they poured forth from my
  heart's understanding.
²⁸Happy those who meditate upon
  these things;
  wise those who take them to
  heart!
²⁹If they put them into practice, they
  can cope with anything,
  for the fear of the LORD is their
  lamp.

A Prayer of Thanksgiving

51 ¹I give you thanks, LORD and
  King,
I praise you, God my savior!
I declare your name, refuge of my
  life,
  ²because you have ransomed my
  life from death;
You held back my body from the pit,
  and delivered my foot from the
  power of Sheol.

You have preserved me from the
  scourge of the slanderous
  tongue,
and from the lips of those who
  went over to falsehood.
You were with me against those who
  rise up against me;

---

the Samaritans centered on Shechem (Nablus) to the north (1 Macc 3:10).
Sirach 50:26 calls the Samaritans the "foolish people," echoing Deuteronomy
32:21. Viewing the Samaritans as mixed-race pagans (2 Kgs 17:24-41), the
returning Jewish exiles refused to let them assist in rebuilding the Jerusalem
temple (Ezra 4:1-3; Neh 3:33-35).

The second postscript (50:27-29) is the author's signature, with an encouragement for readers to practice his teachings.

51:1-12 Hymn of thanksgiving for deliverance

At the opening of the hymn, the sage acclaims the Deity as both savior
and king (Pss 18:47; 145:1). The threat to Ben Sira's life came from a slanderous tongue, stirring up a whispering campaign against him (Jer 20:10). The
danger became a raging fire (Isa 43:2), like the testing spoken of in 2:5.
Mention of the "deep belly of Sheol" (51:5) is reminiscent of the prayer of
Jonah, who regarded his stay inside the great fish as time spent in the belly
of the nether world (Jonah 2:3).

According to 51:6, Ben Sira felt close to death (Ps 88:4), as did St. Paul
in Ephesus, before God rescued him (2 Cor 1:8-10). In his trouble the sage
had the terrible experience of feeling alone, without any human helper (Pss
69:21; 142:5). But then he remembered God's past mercies (Ps 25:6; Lam
3:21-23). Hence, from his humble position he raised his voice to God, just
as the ailing Hezekiah also prayed from the "gates of Sheol" (Isa 38:10). In

³You have rescued me according to your abundant mercy
From the snare of those who look for my downfall,
and from the power of those who seek my life.

From many dangers you have saved me,
⁴from flames that beset me on every side,
From the midst of fire till there was not a whiff of it,
⁵from the deep belly of Sheol,
From deceiving lips and painters of lies,
⁶from the arrows of a treacherous tongue.

I was at the point of death,
my life was nearing the depths of Sheol;
⁷I turned every way, but there was no one to help;
I looked for support but there was none.
⁸Then I remembered the mercies of the LORD,
his acts of kindness through ages past;

For he saves those who take refuge in him,
and rescues them from every evil.

⁹So I raised my voice from the grave;
from the gates of Sheol I cried for help.
¹⁰I called out: LORD, you are my Father,
my champion, my savior!
Do not abandon me in time of trouble,
in the midst of storms and dangers.
¹¹I will always praise your name
and remember you in prayer!

Then the LORD heard my voice,
and listened to my appeal.
¹²He saved me from every evil
and preserved me in time of trouble.
For this reason I thank and praise him;
I bless the name of the LORD.

Ben Sira's Pursuit of Wisdom
¹³When I was young and innocent, I sought wisdom.

51:10 Ben Sira's prayer is direct: "You are my Father" (Isa 63:16; Ps 89:27). Similarly, an apocryphal Qumran prayer of Joseph for deliverance addresses God as "my Father" (4Q372 1.16), while Jesus' prayer in Gethsemane begins: "*Abba*, Father" (Mark 14:36). Sirach 51:11-12 recounts the sage's deliverance in answer to his prayer (Pss 6:9-10; 18:7) and his fulfillment of his earlier pledge by giving thanks to God (Pss 22:23; 69:31). Perhaps in response to this promise of praise, the Cairo Hebrew manuscript here includes a sixteen-line litany of thanksgiving, omitted from all the Greek and Syriac translations.

51:13-30 An alphabetic wisdom poem

Ben Sira ends his book with a twenty-three-line Hebrew alphabetic poem describing his successful quest for wisdom, personified as a woman

¹⁴She came to me in her beauty,
  and until the end I will cultivate
    her.

¹⁵As the blossoms yielded to ripening
  grapes,
  the heart's joy,
My feet kept to the level path
  because from earliest youth I was
    familiar with her.

¹⁶In the short time I paid heed,
  I met with great instruction.
¹⁷Since in this way I have profited,
  I will give my Teacher grateful
    praise.

¹⁸I resolved to tread her paths;
  I have been jealous for the good
    and will not turn back.
¹⁹I burned with desire for her,
  never relenting.

I became preoccupied with her,
  never weary of extolling her.
I spread out my hands to the heavens
  and I came to know her secrets.
²⁰For her I purified my hands;
  in cleanness I attained to her.

At first acquaintance with her,
  I gained understanding
  such that I will never forsake her.
²¹My whole being was stirred to
  seek her;
  therefore I have made her my
    prize possession.
²²The Lᴏʀᴅ has rewarded me with
  lips,
  with a tongue for praising him.

²³Come aside to me, you untutored,
  and take up lodging in the house
  of instruction;

(14:20–15:10). The Psalter makes frequent use of such alphabetic poems (acrostics) where each line starts successively with one of the twenty-two letters of the Hebrew alphabet (e.g., Psalms 111, 112, 145). Here (as in Psalm 25) an extra line is added beginning with the letter *pe*.

Though some scholars have questioned the authorship of this poem, indications that the poem is indeed the work of Ben Sira include his characteristic themes of courting Lady Wisdom (51:13-21; 14:20–15:2) and submitting to her yoke (51:26; 6:24, 30). In fact, 51:13-30 also seems to echo the alphabetic poem concluding the book of Proverbs (Prov 31:10-31). Whereas the poem at the end of Proverbs concerns the valiant woman who embodies the fear of the Lord, Ben Sira's composition is about wisdom, personified as a desirable woman.

Sirach 51:13 describes the sage's youthful search for wisdom (6:18), reminiscent of Solomon's early quest for understanding (1 Kgs 3:7-9; Wis 8:2). According to 51:15, already as a young man Ben Sira knew wisdom (Ps 71:17; Mark 10:20), as did Solomon (47:14). Sirach 51:16 notes that a great advance in understanding came from a small amount of attention (6:19). Whereas 1:6 asks who knows wisdom's subtleties, the sage here declares that he came to know her secrets (51:19). Anyone seeking divine

²⁴How long will you deprive yourself of wisdom's food,
how long endure such bitter thirst?
²⁵I open my mouth and speak of her:
gain wisdom for yourselves at no cost.

²⁶Take her yoke upon your neck;
that your mind may receive her teaching.
For she is close to those who seek her,
and the one who is in earnest finds her.

²⁷See for yourselves! I have labored only a little,
but have found much.
²⁸Acquire but a little instruction,
and you will win silver and gold through her.

²⁹May your soul rejoice in God's mercy;
do not be ashamed to give him praise.
³⁰Work at your tasks in due season,
and in his own time God will give you your reward.

---

understanding needs clean hands and a pure heart (Ps 24:4). Wisdom became Ben Sira's prize possession (Prov 4:7). Like God's servant in the Third Servant Song (Isa 50:4), the sage has been given a tongue to proclaim the divine wisdom and to praise God (39:6).

Then Ben Sira appeals to the uneducated (51:23), echoing the invitation of Lady Wisdom (Prov 1:22-23; 9:4-6). His appeal is that the untutored should lodge in the "house of instruction," a phrase suggesting some kind of educational establishment. In 51:24 Ben Sira asks "how long" his students will lack wisdom's nourishment and drink (Prov 9:5; Isa 55:1).

The image of wisdom's yoke (51:26) develops the thought of an earlier poem (6:24, 30). Sirach 51:26b plays on the Hebrew word *massa*, which means both "burden" (6:21) and "teaching" (Jer 23:33). Wisdom is accessible to those who seek her (Wis 6:12), because God's word is near (Deut 30:14). In practical terms, wisdom will offer material rewards (Prov 8:18), as a result of divine mercy and human diligence (11:1). If the student focuses on the task of acquiring wisdom, God will grant a reward in good time.

REVIEW AIDS AND DISCUSSION TOPICS

Introduction *(pages 5–8)*

1. What are noteworthy features of Ben Sira's teaching?

2. How did Ben Sira become canonical for the Roman Catholic and Greek Orthodox Churches but not for most Protestants or for Jews?

3. Why does the grandson's Greek translation sometimes differ from the Hebrew text?

Grandson's Prologue; 1:1–4:10 Understanding Wisdom *(pages 9–21)*

1. According to the Prologue, why did the grandson decide to translate Ben Sira's book?

2. How is the fear of the Lord related to wisdom (1:11-30)?

3. What is appropriate care for aged parents in our society (3:1-16)?

4. Compare the sage's instruction on humility (3:17-24) with Jesus' teaching on the subject (Matt 18:1-4; Luke 14:7-11).

4:11–6:17 Using Wisdom Personally *(pages 21–25)*

1. For people of today, explain the difference between an appropriate and an inappropriate sense of shame (4:21).

2. In our society, what wisdom is there in listening before talking (5:11-13)?

3. Is Ben Sira's teaching on friendship (6:5-17) too cautious?

6:18–14:19 Applying Wisdom Socially *(pages 25–44)*

1. In the sage's wisdom poem (6:18-37), what helpful advice is given for someone seeking to live wisely?

2. When is it right for good people to avoid friendships with bad people (13:13-17)?

3. What message does Ben Sira's teaching on wealth (13:24–14:19) have for our society?

14:20–23:27 Wisdom in Speech and Thought *(pages 44–67)*

1. Is sin simply a matter of bad human choices (15:11-20)?

2. What opportunities and duties has the Creator given to human beings (17:1-14)?

3. How does God's strength exceed human power (17:29–18:14)?

4. Why does the fool evoke the sage's pity (22:9-12)?

24:1–32:13 Wisdom in Domestic Life *(pages 68–88)*

1. In comparing Sirach 24:1-12 with John 1:1-18, what similarities can you detect?

2. Is the long passage on women (25:13–26:18) entirely outdated, or are some features still relevant today?

3. Explain the connection between Ben Sira's instruction on forgiveness (27:30–28:7) and Jesus' teaching on the topic (Matt 6:14-15; 18:21-35).

4. Why are good table manners important for the wise person (31:12–32:13)?

32:14–38:23 Using Wisdom to Make Good Decisions *(pages 89–105)*

1. What explanation does Ben Sira offer for the balance of good and evil in the world (33:7-15)?

2. What role does travel play in a person's education (34:9-12)?

3. How far can Sirach 34:25-27 be applied to the disparity in wealth between rich and poor nations?

4. How important is discernment when choosing a marriage partner, friend, or advisor (36:26–37:15)?

5. What function has God given to the medical doctor (38:1-15)?

38:24–42:14 Demonstrating the Results of Wisdom *(pages 106–18)*

1. What value do you think the intellectual has, in comparison with the manual worker (38:24–39:11)?

2. If God's works are all good, how can we explain the existence of evil (39:16-35)?

3. According to Ben Sira (40:18-27), what are the truly good things in life?

42:15–50:24 Wisdom in Creation and History *(pages 119–44)*

1. How can the contemplation of creation help us to know the Creator (42:15–43:33)?

2. Which of the biblical characters in chapters 44–46 most appeals to you, and why?

3. Why are some kings praised in chapters 47–49, while others are ignored?

4. Why is the high priest Simeon II significant for Ben Sira?

50:25–51:30 Postscripts and Appendices *(pages 144–48)*

1. How does Ben Sira's prayer of thanksgiving (51:1-12) compare with the prayers of Jonah and Hezekiah (Jonah 2:3-10; Isa 38:10-20)?

2. Is there any general similarity between the figure of personified wisdom in 51:13-30 and the capable wife in Proverbs 31:10-31?

INDEX OF CITATIONS FROM THE
CATECHISM OF THE CATHOLIC CHURCH

The arabic number(s) following the citation refer(s) to the paragraph number(s) in the *Catechism of the Catholic Church*. The asterisk following a paragraph number indicates that the citation has been paraphrased.

Sirach

1:22	2339*	11:14	304*	30:1-2	2223
3:2-6	2218	15:14	1730, 1743	36:17 (36:11)	441*
3:12	2218	17:22	2447*	37:27-31	1809*
3:16	2218	18:30	1809	43:27-28	2129
5:2	1809	21:28	2477*	43:28	300*
5:8	2536	24	721*	48:1	696
7:27-28	2215	27:16	2489*	50:20	433*